TOWARDS A
GENERAL COMPARATIVE
LINGUISTICS

by

JEFFREY ELLIS

UNIVERSITY OF ESSEX

1966

MOUTON & CO.

LONDON · THE HAGUE · PARIS

Printed in The Netherlands.

PREFACE

Thanks are due to Dr. M. A. K. Halliday, Dr. R. Huddleston and Miss J. N. Ure for reading and commenting on the original draft of *Towards a General Comparative Linguistics*.

This book also contains as appendices some of my writings from various periods on the same general subject to which considerable reference is made in the main body of the work; I have to thank Dr. Halliday for suggesting this, the previous publishers of some of the appendices for permission to reprint (see General Note on Appendices), and Professor C. H. van Schooneveld, Editor of *Janua Linguarum*, and Messrs Mouton & Co. for agreeing to publish the whole in the series minor of *Janua Linguarum*.

Edinburgh, July, 1964.   J. ELLIS

CONTENTS

INTRODUCTION

The term "comparative linguistics" in current usage has confused reference and controversial overtones. On the one hand it suggests *linguistique comparée, vergleichende Sprachwissenschaft, сравнительное языкознание,* etc., in less ambiguous English comparative philology or "the comparative – historical method" (less ambiguously still, genetic comparative linguistics), and to many still that is something to be got away from altogether in contemporary linguistics; on the other hand, another kind of comparative linguistics is found avoiding the name by calling itself "contrastive linguistics", and being attacked under the same name by certain comparative philologists.[1]

The present work is an attempt to vindicate comparative linguistics as a part of general linguistics: as all and any linguistics that is comparative; and as a comprehensive discipline with unifying theoretical principles, based on the general theory of general linguistics (general comparative linguistics).

One of these principles is that just as descriptive linguistics is central to general linguistics, inasmuch as one needs to describe languages before doing anything else with them (such as comparing them, or tracing their history, or teaching them, or undertaking Machine Translation, etc., etc.), so comparative descriptive linguistics is central to comparative linguistics, inasmuch as one needs to compare descriptions of languages before doing anything

[1] E.g. in J. Whatmough's paper ("Continental Celtic") at the Second International Congress of Celtic Studies, Cardiff, 1963; cf. S. Andrews and J. Whatmough, "Comparative and Historical Linguistics in America", *Trends in European and American Linguistics 1930–60* (Utrecht, 1963), pp. 58–81: p. 63, ". . . the risk, to comparative and historical studies in general, from contamination due to occasional attempts to apply structural techniques . . ."

else comparative with them (such as tracing their origins, or applying comparison in teaching, or in translation theory, etc., etc.). And this seems sufficient reason for not cutting off comparative descriptive linguistics terminologically from other kinds of comparative linguistics by calling it "contrastive linguistics", or even (which has not the same lexicological objections to it[2]) "confrontational linguistics" *(сопоставительная лингвистпка)*.[3]

Another principle is that the kinds of comparative linguistics need to be classified, according to the ways in which and the purposes for which they compare languages, before their interrelation with comparative descriptive linguistics and with each other can be examined. The first part of this work will therefore briefly enumerate and exemplify the kinds of comparative linguistics, anticipating to some extent their relation to comparative descriptive linguistics. A fuller treatment of partial aspects of this, including the interrelations, will be found elsewhere.[4] The second part will attempt a summary of the methods of comparative descriptive linguistics itself.

---

[2]   One even finds usages like ". . . which features to contrast . . .", meaning not merely which to confront but which to identify with each other.
[3]   The latter names might be of use in the sense of *applied* comparative descriptive linguistics (cf. n. 5), though possibly encouraging the notion that this is the sole *raison d'être* of comparative descriptive linguistics.
[4]   Ellis, "General Linguistics and Comparative Philology", *Lingua*, VII (1958), pp. 134-174 (= Appendix B), "Some Problems in Comparative Linguistics", *Proceedings of the University of Durham Philosophical Society*, Vol. 1, Series B (*Arts*), (1961), No. 7, pp. 54-62 (= Appendix C), "Possible Comparisons of Balkan and North-West European Linguistic Community, with Reference to System-Reduction Method of Quantification", *Славянска Филология*, Том III (Sofia, 1963), pp. 291-299 (= Appendix F); also M. A. K. Halliday, "Some Aspects of Systematic Description and Comparison in Grammatical Analysis", *Studies in Linguistic Analysis*, ed. J. R. Firth, (Oxford, 1957), pp. 54-67, "Linguistics and Machine Translation", *Zeitschrift für Phonetik, Sprachwissenschaft und Kommunikationsforschung*, 15 (1962), pp. 145–158. For the theory of descriptive linguistics see Appendix A.

KINDS OF COMPARATIVE LINGUISTICS

1.0 CLASSIFICATION OF COMPARATIVE LINGUISTICS

The following classification of the main lines of division of comparative linguistics is provisional; for example it might be considered that dialectology, etc. (here 1.34) should be classed with historical linguistics (here 1.22) as being equally comparison for all purposes of tongues related in a special way (parts of one more comprehensive language) – for the arguments against this consideration see below, 1.13, 1.134 and 1.34.

1.01   General: methodology, interrelations, etc.

02   All-purpose comparison
021   Descriptive (synchronic)
0211 Comparative descriptive linguistics of particular languages
0212 Linguistic typology
022   Historical
0221 Comparison of etats (special case of 0211)
0222 Atomistic (as opp. systemic)
0223 Comparison of histories
0224 Typology of change (0223 and 0224 related as 0211 and 0212
03   Comparison with specific purpose (Specialized Comparative Linguistics)
031   Linguistic theory of translation
032   Genetic comparative linguistics (comparative philology)
033   Languages in contact (contact comparative linguistics)
0331 Linguistic theory of bilingualism
0332 Loaning in general ⎫
0333 Areal convergence ⎬ Partial-genetic comparative linguistics

034   Dialectology, etc.
       (Institutional linguistics an ancillary study at many points.)

1.1 GENERAL COMPARATIVE LINGUISTICS

The general principles of comparative linguistics cover what, other than the specific techniques of comparative descriptive linguistics, is common to the various kinds: the notion of comparison in general and its application to languages, the *quantification* of comparison, the concept and techniques of the comparison of comparisons and its quantification (generalization of the quantifications of individual comparisons).

The notion of comparison of course comprises resemblance and contrast (cf. n. 2 on p. 12). The detailed examination of the notion in linguistics will draw on the logic and methodology of comparison in the sciences in general (reference being made to such principles as Mill's Joint Method of Agreement and Difference, etc.). Distinction must however be made between "comparison" of linguistic elements, which may occur in the descriptive linguistics of one language (commutation, transformation, etc.), and comparison in *comparative* linguistics, where the objects of comparison are different languages or tongues (and language-varieties (see 1.34)) as wholes, or elements in them.

Quantification is accordingly of proportions of resemblance and difference within a pair of languages or their parts (systems (2.22), levels (1.32, 2.1), etc.), or, in texts, of proportions of occurrences of an item (or category) in which items (or categories) of the other language correspond to it. On the uneven development to date of quantitative methods in kinds of comparative linguistics cf. "Possible Comparisons", p. 296, n. 39 (= Appendix F, p. 149) (,and 1.32 below).

Comparison of comparisons introduces a new dimension of "meta"-relation. "Metacomparison" itself and its applications are treated below (2.3, 2.222, 1.212, 1.32, 1.333, etc.); here, as to its theoretical nature, it needs to be pointed out that this second-degree comparison is unlike, as regards the complexity of the range of possible objects compared, the comparisons that are being compared: whatever the object being compared in these (texts (2.21), systems (2.22), items (1.222, 1.32), etc.), once quantified the comparisons are all susceptible of one general method of "meta-comparison".

General comparative linguistics also includes the consideration of the differences between and interrelations of the kinds:

1.11 *Relations of General Comparative Linguistics*

All-purpose comparative linguistics and comparative linguistics with specific purposes differ in that the first abstracts from purposes and ways of comparison, the second abstracts from purposes, the third comprises kinds defined by purpose[1] (study of translation and bilingualism, of genetic relation, etc.) and only secondarily by kind of tongue compared (ones in translation-relation (in a given case), ones genetically related (or possibly so), ones in contact-relations, dialects and other varieties of one language); they interrelate inasmuch as all-purpose comparison and comparison with specific purpose draw on general comparative linguistics, comparison with specific purpose draws on all-purpose comparison (specific kinds of the one on those of the other, see below).

1.12 *All-purpose Comparative Linguistics*

All-purpose comparative linguistics is sub-divided primarily by kind of tongue compared ("descriptive", i.e. any tongues; "historical", i.e. periods of one language), then by scope of objects of comparison (particular/typological), and finally by ways of comparison.

These interrelate: descriptive with historical as providing the general methods for this as a special case; particular with typo-

---

[1] Note that "applied" (scil. to pedagogical purposes) linguistics forms a separate dimension of classification of linguistics from the simple/comparative dimension (and includes an intersection with the latter in distinguishing, within general applied linguistics, applied simple descriptive linguistics and applied comparative linguistics (itself dividing into general applied comparative linguistics, applied comparative descriptive linguistics, applied linguistics of translation and of bilingualism, etc.)).

logical as providing the data to generalize from; within particular comparative descriptive linguistics, see 2.2; within historical, atomistic (insofar as this traditional sense of historical linguistics can be incorporated into scientific general linguistics) presupposes comparison of etats, comparison of histories presupposes comparison of etats and atomistic, typology of change presupposes comparison of histories.

1.13 *Specialized Comparative Linguistics*

Comparative linguistics with specific purpose is sub-divided according to purpose. (Dialectology, etc., which would appear to differ from comparative descriptive linguistics of any tongues only in kind of tongue compared, as historical linguistics does, may be regarded as having specific purposes, and differs also as regards the discreteness of the tongues concerned (see below, 1.134 and 1.34).)

1.131 *Linguistic Theory of Translation*

Linguistic theory of translation draws on particular comparative descriptive linguistics. It also reacts back on it in providing both data and a practical means of contextualization (see 2.1), and more particularly rank-bound translation (see 1.31, 2.21), and in treating the question of asymmetry of relation between languages in translation-relation (see 2.1, 2.21 and 2.2223). It also draws on, and reacts back on, linguistic theory of bilingualism.

1.132 *Genetic Comparative Linguistics*

Genetic comparative linguistics has a more complex relation to all-purpose comparative linguistics, not straightforward application of it, and provision of material to it, as theory of translation to particular comparative descriptive linguistics, but presupposition of the results of both particular comparative descriptive linguistics and historical linguistics, and also possible drawing on typology (both synchronic and historical).[2] As a case of comparative lin-

---

[2] Cf. *Proceedings of 7th International Congress of Linguists London 1952*, pp. 109–10, 116–7; *Proceedings of 8th International Congress of Linguists Oslo 1957*: Jakobson, "Typological Studies and Their Contribution to Historical Comparative Linguistics"; *GLCP*, p. 171, n. 134 (Appendix B, p. 108, n. 133).

guistics with specific purpose, both as concept and in quantification, it exhibits peculiarities of probability and of systemicness (see 1.32).

1.133 *Languages in Contact*

The concept of *partial-genetic* comparative linguistics binds together genetic comparative linguistics and contact comparative linguistics 332 and 333. The distinction between discrete language or tongue and part thereof belongs in the linguistic theoretical fundamentals underlying both linguistic theory of bilingualism and the contrast of history and dialect in 1.13, 1.134, 1.34, and is crucial to institutional linguistics.

1.1331 *Areal Convergence.*

– More specifically, the comparative linguistics of areal convergence falls in some ways between comparative descriptive linguistics of any languages and genetic comparative linguistics of languages related as wholes (see "Possible Comparisons", pp. 295–6 (= Appendix F, pp. 148–49), and cf. below, 1.333).

1.134 *Dialectology, etc.*

Dialectology, etc. combines the application of comparative descriptive linguistics to dialects and other language-varieties (see 1.34), which in itself would be a mere case of all-purpose comparison, with accounting for them, in their existence and diversity, as a case of genetic comparative linguistics, and in their use, drawing on theory of bilingualism and as subject of institutional linguistics.

1.14 *Institutional Linguistics*

Institutional linguistics[3] as such is (like "applied" above, n. 1) a separate dimension of classification of linguistics, and not a kind of comparative linguistics specifically (though in a way that "applied"

---

[3] See T. Hill, "Institutional Linguistics", *Orbis*, VII (1958), pp. 441–455; also J. Ellis, "Some Recent Work on German Grammar", *Archivum Linguisticum*, XIII, pp. 33 ff., pp. 40–42, "Linguistic Sociology and Institutional Linguistics", *Linguistics*, 19 (1965), pp. 5-20.

linguistics does not, its field by definition presupposes more than one tongue under description, hence comparison). But its findings are essential to dialectology, etc., linguistic theory of bilingualism (and hence of translation), areal convergence, and genetic comparative linguistics, as much as their findings and techniques to it.

1.2 ALL-PURPOSE COMPARATIVE LINGUISTICS

To exemplify the kinds of this, let us take the English "I've come", "he's come", and (anticipating 2.1, 2.2212, 2.2221) the more usual equivalent in various languages "je suis venu", "ich bin gekommen", etc.

1.21 *Descriptive (Synchronic)*

Here the examples will be from any languages of any periods, e.g. "veni" (in any historical period of Latin), not necessarily tongues in historical relation as etats of a language, e.g. "I have come" – "ic cwōm"; "je suis venu" – "veni".

1.211 *Particular Comparative Descriptive Linguistics*
This is treated in detail in 2. Here will be given introductory examples.

1.2111 *Linear or Textual Comparison* (see 2.21). – Here a text or utterance or part thereof, e.g. "I have come", is compared with the corresponding text in another language, e.g. "je suis venu", correspondences (of categories and their exponents (including formal items)) being stated at all points on the (formal) scales of (grammatical) rank (see 2.21, 1.31), exponence (see 2.21) and (grammatical) delicacy (see 2.1, 2.21), e.g. (formal items) "to *I* + the person-number of *have* corresponds *je* + the person-number of *suis* + the number of *venu*", "to *have* + past participle in *come* corresponds *être* + past participle in *venu*", "nothing corresponds to gender of *venu*", "to lexical item *come* corresponds lexical item *venir*".

1.2112 *Systemic Comparison.* (see 2.22). – Here the instantial correspondences of items (categories or exponents) in texts are generalized as potential correspondences (with or without further specification of relative frequencies) of terms in systems, e.g. "to *I* as a term in a five-term system of personal pronouns corresponds *je* as a term in a six-term system", "to *he* as a term in a three-term system of natural gender (or four-term system of natural gender and number in third person) corresponds partly *il* as a term in a two-term system of grammatical gender (or four-term system of grammatical gender and number in third person)".

1.212 *Linguistic Typology*

Here comparison is no longer of pairs or combination of pairs of languages, but in principle all possible languages are classified according to salient features or patterns of combination of features (involving "metacomparison", cf. 2.3).

Although attempts at typological classification are as old as modern linguistics in the wide sense, no satisfactory general scheme of linguistic typology yet exists, and clearly such establishment of a comprehensive framework must await further comparative description of individual languages, and evaluation of "saliency" of features and of their interconnection (cf. n. 7). But, although long discredited or neglected, the subject has lately received renewed attention from reputable scholars.[4]

Traditional typology could be represented by examples like: "isolating" (better "grouping" (Meriggi)) Chinese $w\ŏ^1$ $l\ái^2$ le^3;[5] "agglutinative" Turkish gel^2 di^3 m^1; "inflectional" Latin $v\ēn^{23}$ $\bar{i}^{13}$, where inflectional is distinguished by variety of exponence and variety of categories expounded by the same exponent, and by the extent of cumulation of categories in one exponent, and both inflectional and agglutinative from "isolating" by the grammatical rank at which categories are expounded or by the relative phonological rank of the exponent, and by the non-optionality of grammatical categories (also, and also distinguishing "stem-isolating"

---

[4] E.g. Jakobson, Bazell, Greenber (continuing Sapir – Martinet (*op. cit.* in n. 7 below), p. 66, n. 2), Martinet (cf. n. 7).

[5] For the transcription see n. 65 on p. 54.

from fully isolating, by the degree of affixation in formation of lexical items).[6] Such a statement can be based on, as one possible generalization from, the kind of comparisons in 2., but is clearly inadequate as a general characterization of the grammar, let alone other levels,[7] of languages.

1.22 *Historical Linguistics*

This differs from 1.21 only inasmuch as the identity of the tongues under comparison, being etats de langue of one language, provides certain additional criteria for and aids to comparison. E.g., formal items being exponentially identifiable with each other (cf. 1.32), phonologically or graphologically, it is possible, in many cases, to proceed from "common exponents", e.g. OE *ic*, ModE *I*, and compare the differing formal meanings, e.g. "ic hit eom" beside "it's me" (but it is possible to make the "exponential" identification only because of a high degree of correspondence to begin with (especially between the chronologically closer etats) in formal and contextual meaning (cf. 1.32), e.g. parallel environments of *ic/I* like *cwōm/have come*). Again, (in arriving at such equation of instantial meanings) contextualization is specially facilitated by the continuity of literature and other traditions embodied in the successive stages of the language, e.g. "sumer is icumen in", insofar as still understood (and the common *mis*understanding, as "a-coming", illustrates the pitfalls that also complicate the special situation of *historic-*

---

[6] "On Comparative Descriptive Linguistics", *Studia Linguistica in honorem Acad. S. Mladenov*, (Sofia, 1957), pp. 555–565 p. 564 (= Appendix G, p. 169).

[7] Cf. A. Martinet, *A Functional View of Language* (Oxford, 1962), pp. 66–102 ("Linguistic Typology"), pp. 67, 73, 87–90, 98–102: while phonology may be typologized, form and especially meaning is central. For lexis in typology cf. M. A. K. Halliday, "Lexis as a Linguistic Level" (to appear in *In Memory of J. R. Firth*, London, 1966 *Volume*): "...lexical series...*oaktree, ashtree, planetree, beechtree* presumably do operate in the same [collocational] set, while *inkstand, bandstand, hallstand, grandstand* almost certainly do not.... Equivalence or non-equivalence between series and set is an interesting feature of lexical typology: one would predict that in Chinese, for example, practically all such series do form sets (with an unmarked member), whereas in Malay and English they very often do not."

ally associated data), links, through generations of speakers, "hē ist (ge)cumen" and "he has come".[8]

This difference (from 1.21) does not indeed go as far as that of 1.34 (despite Catford's inclusion of "temporal provenance" (as far apart as ModE and OE) under linguistic variety). Etats de langue are institutionally independent of each other as dialects and other synchronic varieties are not – always remembering, of course, the (diachronically one-way) appearance of earlier etats as register-material (cf. 1.34) in later ones.[9]

1.221 *Comparison of Etats*

Here the etats are compared by just the same procedures as languages in 1.21, e.g. *ic cwōm* with *I have come.*

1.222 *Atomistic*

This is "historical linguistics" (or philology of one language) as traditionally understood, where instead of systemic comparison of one etat (itself synchronically described) with another (1.221) individual items are traced through diachronically (e.g. *ic* > (under conditions) *i* > (under conditions) /i:/ > /ai/), but here with the difference that the identification of the item as a term in a system (cf. 1.32) at each stage (1.221) is presupposed, and the developments and their conditions ultimately integrated into systematic wholes[10] (e.g. the systemic connections of the succession (and its phonological conditioning) *ic* > *ich/i*; *i* > i:/i; i: > *I*).

1.223 *Comparison of Histories*

Here 1.22 reunites further with 1.21 in comparing the comparison[11] of etats (as in 1.221) or of their items (as in 1.222) in one

---

[8] The first applies to a lesser degree also to closely related languages like English and German, the second not appreciably. An example of the limitations of the first within one language would be OE *-nde, -ynge*, ModE *-ing.*

[9] Cf. N. Bachtin, "English Poetry in Greek", *The Link*, nos. 1 & 2 (Oxford, 1938–9).

[10] Cf. A. Martinet, *A Functional View of Language* (Oxford, 1962), pp. 134–160 ("Linguistic Evolution").

[11] For comparison of comparisons cf. 2.3.

language with that in another, e.g. comparing the development of OE *be* or *have* with past participle to ModE "past in" term in tense system expounded by *have* with past participle with the development of Vulgar Latin or Old French construction with past participle to Modern French *avoir* or (with a small number of verbs) *être* + past participle.

(Note that insofar as this particular example involves a question of common origin (Latin influence on OE) it is the subject-matter of 1.33 (1.332 or 1.333) and 1.32; in 1.223 the languages whose history is compared can, like those in 1.21, be any two languages irrespective of genetic relation of language or part of language.)

1.224 *Typology of Change*

This would have the same relation to 1.223 as 1.22 to 1.21, and is all the more a potential rather than established part of comparative linguistics. It will moreover present difficulties of demarcation on the one side from establishment of general laws of change (as attempted e.g. by E. Reifler for semantic associations) or "panchronic" tendencies, on the other from "synchronic" typology (1.212), which at its most general embraces long periods of history of any one language or family.[12] But a possible example of its detailed subject-matter would be the classification of *developments* like the origination of the construction of the "I have come" type on the one hand, and on the other of those of the *lái le*, Scottish Gaelic *tha air tighinn*, and other types.

1.3 SPECIALIZED COMPARATIVE LINGUISTICS

1.31 *Linguistic Theory of Translation*

The linguistic theory of translation is part of theory of translation in general.[13]

The application of linguistic theory to the field of translation may be exemplified by the process of "rank-bound translation"

[12] E.g. H. Wagner, *Das Verbum in den Sprachen der Britischen Inseln* (Tübingen, 1959).
[13] See J. C. Catford, *A Linguistic Theory of Translation* (OUP), Halliday, *LMT* (n. 4, p. 12), Ellis, *op. cit.* n. 6, p. 20, above.

originated in "Linguistics and Machine Translation", described there (pp. 151–2) as follows: –

". . . sentences are shown segmented into their successive lower units: clauses, groups, words and morphemes, with each boundary implying all these below it (a group boundary must also be a word and morpheme boundary, and so on). . . ."

"Each sentence is then 'translated' at each rank . . .: first each morpheme is taken separately, then each word, and so on. In each case the . . . equivalent *item* is one which might turn out – at a guess: the counting has not been done [but cf. n. 21] – to be the most frequent translation equivalent *at that rank*: the one which would be the first choice for entry in a bilingual 'dictionary' of morphemes, words, groups, etc. Similarly the grammatical *pattern* chosen is that which might be the most frequent translation equivalent at the rank concerned. (The concept 'most frequent translation equivalent' for a *grammatical item* in isolation, such as English 'the' or '-ing', is however inapplicable; such items are here symbolized 'X' until their incorporation into higher units.) If we start from the morpheme (cf. n. 14), we can follow the translation step by step up the rank scale, each equivalent being adjusted as it finds itself co-occurring with certain other items, in a certain grammatical relation, in the unit next above. So for example Chinese *tie*, as a morpheme, would most frequently be translated 'iron'; when it is taken as part of the word into which it enters, this translation is the one most likely to appear (as when it is a word on its own, or in the words *tieqi* 'ironware' or *shengtie* 'cast iron'; elsewhere other equivalents must be chosen (*gangtie* 'steel', *tielu* 'railway'). Each step can be regarded as a process in which the equivalent is retained unless positive contrary indications are found in the next unit.

"It appears clearly that, while equivalence can be stated, in terms of probabilities, for all ranks, translation in the accepted sense does not occur below the rank of the clause, and a good translation needs to be based on the sentence as its unit. So-called 'literal' translation is, roughly, translation at group rank, or at a mixture of group and word."

To this scale of rank is added in the example below a line "above"[14] the grammatical units, "text" (T).[15] (Halliday's "sentence as unit of good translation" is more true of non-literary (and non-conversational) texts.) Note that the rank scale is that of the language being translated; the translating items need not be exponents of the corresponding unit.

Example (as below, 2.21) from English: French (actually English ← French,[16] cf. 2.21 2.2221, 2.2223),[17] these being the only well-known languages as yet described according to the theory here followed in the kind of detail called for by adequate comparison.[18]

	||| Les carottes	sont cuites, || comme	on dit. ||| [19]
M	X carrot X X cook X X X say X[20]
W	X carrots are cooked as X says
G	the (·634[21]) carrots are cooked as one says
C	the carrots (·775) are cooked as they say
S	It's served up on a plate, as they say.
T	We've got it, as they say, served up on a plate.

[14] Represented by sequence below, in view of the "lexicographical" nature of the process (cf. 2.21).

[15] Abstracting from the possible divisions of "text" above the grammatical rank scale, such as "paragraph", cf. M. A. K. Halliday, "Categories of the Theory of Grammar", *Word*, 17 (1961), pp. 241–292 (p. 255, n. 30).

[16] The fact that the rank-bound translation in the example given is also in the same direction is coincidental (cf. 2.2223).

[17] F. Mauriac, *Thérèse*, trsl. Gerard Hopkins, (London, Penguin, 1959), p. 11, 1.19, *Thérèse Desqueyroux* (1927) (Paris, Grasset, 1960), p. 2, 1.9. (R. Huddleston, "A Descriptive and Comparative Analysis of Texts in French and English: an Application of Grammatical Theory", Ph. D. thesis submitted Edinburgh, 1963, p. 299.)

[18] On the problem of arriving at a terminology, and notation, of categories of different languages (*not* comparative linguistics but (comparative metalinguistics) application of the descriptive theory to different languages) cf. 2.1. (Huddleston's (p. 303) description of English (nominal group) slanted for comparative purposes is not necessarily followed here.)

[19] The analysis (of the French) is Huddleston's. The symbols |||, ||, | and space represent sentence-, clause-, group- and word-boundaries (morpheme-boundaries are not attempted in this way here, though reflected in the translation (M), French (and English) presenting difficulties in segmentation (cf. Halliday, *LMT*, p. 251)).

[20] At morpheme rank each X stands for one or more grammatical items.

[21] For explanation of the figures in parenthesis see 2.2221.

For further examples of rank-bound translation (in various applications) see below, 2.21.0, 2.2221, and Appendix D.

1.32 *Genetic Comparative Linguistics*

This may be represented, very schematically and inadequately, using the example of 1.2, as follows (it may also be partially re-presented in a way that anticipates 2.21, see below): –

English	German	etc.		Pr. Germanic
come-/came	komm-/kam-	etc.	→	*$k^we/a/um$-
	etc.			etc.
Pr. Germanic	Latin	etc.		Pr. Indo-European
*$k^we/a/um$-	ven-	etc.	→	*g^uem-/g^uom-/g^nm-
	etc.			etc.

One reason for the inadequacy of this representation is that it does not, except by "etc.", show the magnitude of the data involved (in any language, and number of languages) before the statement about any one item can be (firmly) made, nor the application of certain principles of probability absent from non-genetic kinds of comparative linguistics, according to which the (firm) statement about any one item need never be of an absolute certainty but the statement about the language of increasing probability as more statements (of probability) about items are made.[22]

Another is that it does not make explicit the particular way in which the levels of linguistic analysis (cf. n. 1, p. 33) enter into this kind of comparative linguistics (cf. n. 2, p. 33). This may be illustrated by extending the statement of minimum correspondences (1.2111, elaborated in 2.21) between texts, of (formal) items that would co-vary in minimal changes of the text, e.g. "to lexical item *come* corresponds lexical item *ven(i)*-", to statement of minimum correspondences (graphologically (which capitalizes on historical orthography) or (observably or inductively) phonologically (phonemic or distinctive-feature[23])) of (exponential) items that would

---

[22] See "General Linguistics and Comparative Philology", pp. 144–5, 150 (Appendix B, pp. 81–2,87).
[23] See *GLCP*, p. 156 (Appendix B, p. 93), "Some Problems in Comparative Linguistics", p. 57 (Appendix C, p. 119).

co-vary in the languages in general, in different sets of formal items (basically of morpheme rank[24]) for each correspondence, e.g. "to c- (when from $*k^w$-) corresponds v-", "to -m- corresponds -n- before $*\mathbf{i}$", and of this to formal items that never correspond (textually, i.e.) contextually (e.g. *guest, hostis*), provided that the assumed development of contextual meanings is sufficiently probable,[25] and basing on a sufficient quantity of such exponential correspondences, of appropriate ("relatively relevant") kinds of formal items, a statement of genetic relation of the languages as wholes; where the role of the levels is that phonological exponence coupled with contextual meaning provides the evidence for identification of individual formal items,[26] and that the distinction of grammar from lexis and within lexis of a certain kind of contextual meanings[27] (descriptive formal properties of which have yet to be investigated) provides the criterion of relative relevance of items and correspondences to identity and relation of the language as a whole.

Thus within the level of form genetic comparative linguistics differs from comparative descriptive linguistics as regards *systemicness* in that items while *identified* (descriptively) as terms in systems are *compared* as atomistic items (cf. 1.222), i.e. irrespective of synchronic interconnections of formal and hence of contextual meaning (though not of relatedness of contextual meaning, nor, more particularly, of possibility of partial systemic statement of items *reconstructed* (e.g. of $*-\mathbf{i}$- as *Aktionsart* suffix)).[28]

Both probabilities and "sufficient quantities" (of given kinds of

---

[24] *GLCP*, p. 143 with n. 32 (Appendix B, p. 80 with n. 31) and *SPCL*, p. 62 (Appendix C, p. 125); cf. Mann in n. 25 below.

[25] or partially attested, e.g. the "stranger" meaning of the OE and OLat (v. Cic. *Off*. 1, 12, 37) forms of our example. Cf. *GLCP*, p. 144 (and p. 163, nn. 116, 117) (Appendix B, p. 81)(and p. 100, nn.). S.E.Mann, *Language*, 28 (1952), p. 40 (referring to *Language*, 26, 1950, p. 379), insists on "regarding the complete correspondence of whole words" (presumably as lexical items) "as the only sound evidence for etymology".

[26] *GLCP*, pp. 142–5 (Appendix B, pp. 79–82).

[27] *GLCP*, p. 148 with n. 56 (Appendix B, p. 85 with n. 55).

[28] *GLCP*, pp. 151, 159–60 (Appendix B, pp. 88, 96–7), *SPCL*, p. 58 (Appendix C, p. 120).

items) suggest the need for exact principles of *quantification* of genetic comparative linguistic method, although precisely because of its probabilistic nature genetic comparative linguistics may be said to have been essentially[29] established before such quantification has been devised.[30]

The question of such general quantification for *establishment* of genetic relation at all is irrespective of the validity or invalidity of the *glottochronological*, and specifically *lexicostatistical*, method for measuring (in the absence of extra-linguistic historical evidence) the *time-depth* of such relation.[31]

The general quantification involves a special case of "meta-comparison", see 2.3.

On the relation between genetic comparative linguistics and dialectology etc. see (1.134, 1.14 and) 1.34.

1.33 Languages in Contact (Contact Comparative Linguistics)

As a comprehensive concept, contact comparative linguistics is complementary to genetic comparative linguistics in treating, instead of the axis of time along which languages related as wholes have (through spatial etc. separation) diverged, the axis of spatial contact through which (in time) languages (irrespective of genetic relation as wholes) may converge (to a lesser degree, with less intimate contact, through translation, cultural influence, etc.; to a greater degree, in protracted close contiguity).[32]

1.331 Linguistic Theory of Bilingualism

Contact of languages as institutional wholes takes place through

[29]   as regards the central core of convincing instances; cf. *GLCP*, pp. 170–2 (Appendix B, pp. 107–8).
[30]   For references see E. Pulgram, "The Nature and Use of Proto-Languages", *Lingua*, X (1961), pp. 18–37 (p. 25, n. 8); A. S. C. Ross, "Philological Probability Problems", *Journal of the Royal Statistical Society*, series B (*Methodological*), XII (1950), pp. 19–59 (pp. 19–30). Cf. Appendix E, n. 11, and 1.1 above.
[31]   Cf. Ellis, *Proceedings of Seventh International Congress of Linguists 1952*, pp. 106–7. For other references see D. H. Hymes, *Current Anth.* 1:5–44, 1960 (referred to in *Mathematical Aspects* (reference in n. 45 below, p. 46), p. 187). Cf. also the reference in n. 27 above.
[32]   See U. Weinreich, *Languages in Contact* (New York, 1953, reprint 1963). Also (and also on pidgin-creole contact: convergence producing new language) J. Ellis, *op. cit.*, n. 3 above.

individuals, groupings of individuals (cultural elites, travellers, migrants, etc.), or in cases of wholesale replacement or large-scale convergence, whole communities. The former may have results only for the individual and not at all for the language of the community, but all are subject to the principles of linguistic behaviour of individuals involving more than one language with some degree of mastery, bilingual (trilingual, etc.) behaviour.[33]

The linguistic effects of imperfect bilingual activity of the individual, "interference", may be exemplified by German-speakers' "I have come" for English "I came" or "I came there" for English "I got there".

1.332 *Loaning in General*

The most universal result of linguistic contact is borrowing of individual items (resulting in genetic relation of small parts of languages, established partly by the item (-accumulation) methods of 1.32). Lexical borrowing (of exponents or merely of patterns of exponential structure or of meaning (calques)) may be classified into "intimate" and "cultural" borrowing,[34] e.g. *arrive* is (now at least) "intimate", *venue* is "cultural". Under the same conditions as "cultural" (lexical) borrowing may occur also transfer of grammatical structures[35] (also into the language as a whole, if e.g. the French origin of German uvular *r* is accepted, phonic items).

1.333 *Areal Convergence*

Under particular conditions (of protracted close geographical contiguity of language-communities) where there will in any case be "intimate" lexical borrowing on a large scale, there may also occur convergence (as well as in phonological systems or phonic substance) in the systems of grammatical contextual meaning (but not (in general), in distinction from the evidence for genetic relation of whole languages (1.32), common exponents of one kind of gram-

---

[33] See Weinrich, also J. C. Catford's work on bilingualism.
[34] L. Bloomfield, *Language*, Chapters 25 and 26.
[35] Weinreich, including in individual bilinguals.

matical morphemes[36]),[37] which can usually be shown to be a case
of borrowing (grammatical calquing) from one language to the
other(s).[38]

For example, ("literary") Bulgarian and Turkish translate "he
has come" in one of (at least) two ways, depending on whether the
contextual meaning (in registers where the question can arise) involves the speaker's own witnessing of the event referred to (if so,
дойде, *geldi*, if not дошел (е), *gelmiş(tir)*); moreover, the pattern
of the exponence in the verbal group, both structure, perfect
participle (-л, *-miş*) with or without *be*, and systemic relation to
the categories of the verbal group (e.g. in both languages third
person contextual distinction between with and without *be*), is in
virtually complete (in third person complete) correspondence, and
among Bulgarian dialects most so in those of areas that had densest
Turkish colonization.[39] This is but one example of the extensive
and intricate patterns of resemblance connecting in varying degrees
all the Balkan languages.[40]

1.34 *Dialectology, etc.*

So far comparison has been of what may be termed "institutionally
independent tongues". By "tongue"[41] is understood a variety of
language (a language or dialect) that is "linguistically independent"

[36]   *GLCP*, p. 146 with n. 42 (Appendix B, p. 83 with n. 41).
[37]   The total effect of the grammatical and lexical convergence may be represented by examples of rank-bound translation (1.31) from languages with
widespread convergence (e.g. Rumanian and Bulgarian) into any one language
(say English) differing less at less high ranks than that from other languages.
See Appendix D.
[38]   This is now a majority view on the question of origination of "convergence
areas" – which may affect the nomenclature of the phenomenon – see "Possible
Comparisons of Balkan and North-West European Linguistic Community . . .",
pp. 291–3 (Appendix F, pp. 142–44), and to the reference to Martinet there, add
A Functional View of Language, pp. 70–73 (on the association with "typology" cf.
GLCP, nn. 51, 139 (Appendix B, nn. 50, 138). One difficulty in investigating
origination is that in the absence of common phonological exponents part of
the method of 1.32 and of part of 1.332 does not apply (cf. *GLCP*, p. 172
(Appendix B, p. 109)).
[39]   Ellis, *Seventh Congress*, p. 125.
[40]   See "Possible Comparisons" and references there.
[41]   T. Hill, "Institutional Linguistics", *Orbis*, VII (1958), pp. 441–455.

in the sense that it can constitute the total linguistic repertory of a speaker or community and demands its own analysis at all levels. Other, less radically distinguished, varieties will be varieties of one kind or another *within* the tongue or tongues of one speaker (registers[42]) or community (local or social varieties, as well as registers), analysable, partly (in a way that distinct tongues are not (cf. Hill, pp. 450–2)), in association with each other. The general scope of the term "dialect" is in technical usage (as indeed is particular application of other terms[43]) a matter of controversy (Hill, p. 452); here, to avoid ambiguity, when a local (or social) variety ceases to be a tongue (and is describable as "accent", particular local (or social) usages, etc.) it will not be termed "dialect". There is in any case a cline, between language and register, with the other terms between, representable by the following diagram, and along this given linguistic material may move during the history of one or more generations (cf. n. 45).

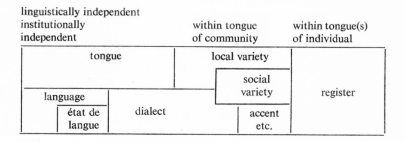

linguistically independent institutionally independent			within tongue of community	within tongue(s) of individual
tongue			local variety	register
language			social variety	
état de langue		dialect	accent etc.	

"Dialectology, etc." is concerned with the comparative linguistic study of dialects and other varieties less than a language. Its relation to genetic comparative linguistics (1.32) is that the latter is concerned with the situation after tongues have ceased to be dialects of the same language, but to a considerable extent they share methods and throw light on each other (e.g. in the "areal linguistics"

---

[42] Ellis, "On Contextual Meaning", to be published in *In Memory of J. R. Firth*, nn. 23 and 24.
[43] E.g. Hill, pp. 450–2, assumes to be discrete tongues varieties of language with considerable overlap by implying that Educated Colloquial English of Scotland with Scots lexis is 100% English not Scots.

application of "linguistic geography" to relations of languages within families).[44] An important difference is that between tongues that are still dialects of the same language,[45] borrowing (cf. 1.332 and 1.333) can take place *at all levels* (contrast 1.333 and 1.32) on such a scale as to merit rather the term "(linguistic) osmosis", and *as long as not distinct languages* (in a linguistic, not institutional, sense, i.e. beyond a threshold of comprehensibility) (cf. n. 45) they can develop either divergently or, "convergently", into social dialects, new local varieties, social varieties, or even register-material.

Examples of local dialect becoming social dialect are koines and "standard languages".[46] An example of a social variety that is not a linguistically independent tongue is the kind of English ("U"[47]) associated with RP at the phonic levels.

An example of some of the dimensions of register-distinction[48] might be "he's come" towards one end of the dimensions of formality (casual) and mode (spoken or other personal interchange), "his arrival is attested" at the other extreme of these and in a particular (technical discourse) role-variety or genre (and probably field, say history).

In principle, registers as much as other varieties are susceptible of descriptive comparison (e.g. "to *have* + past participle in *come* corresponds *be attested*").

They may also figure in the descriptive comparison of tongues generally, as a possible, and more or less delicate, limit on the data;

[44] Cf. *GLCP*, c. p. 149 (Appendix B, c. p. 85), or in Pulgram, *op. cit.*, the implied false conceptions of institutional linguistics and dialectology that would underlie the expressed view that proto-languages of proto-languages undermine the original protolanguages (cf. Appendix E).

[45] *SPCL*, p. 57, n.16 (Appendix C, p. 117); *GLCP*, pp. 148–9 (Appendix B, pp. 85–86).

[46] Hill, *op. cit.*, pp. 443–4.

[47] Borrowing of the identifying term from Ross does not imply acceptance of his distinction U/non-U as the cut of primary delicacy in British-English variety-system. (J. Trim's use of "U" at the phonetic level, distinguished from "RP", is a more delicate distinction within RP as understood here.)

[48] Ellis, "On Contextual Meaning", n. 24.

in linguistic study of translation;[49] in rank-bound translation (1.31), either as conditioning the translation of particular items[50] or (as in descriptive comparison) providing the framework of data of the whole (e.g. in a biblical text on the basis of statistics from the Bible alone).

[49] See J.N. Ure, "Types of Translation and Translatability", *Proceedings of the 3rd International Congress of the International Federation of Translators, Bad Godesberg*, 1959 (Oxford, 1963), pp. 136–146, especially p. 144.
[50] e.g. (John 3. 14, cf. Appendix D, p. 129) items translated "Moses", "snake", "desert" up to group rank, at clause rank translated "Moses", "serpent", "wilderness".

COMPARATIVE DESCRIPTIVE LINGUISTICS

2.1 LEVELS IN COMPARISON AND CRITERIA OF COMPARISON

All levels of linguistic analysis[1] can and should be included in comparison,[2] though in general each only in comparison with the same level in the other language: one possible exception (depending on application of the term level to demilevels[3]) is, within the primary level of form, between the demilevels of grammar and lexis, where a given contextual meaning is expressed grammatically in one language and lexically in another.[4] (For the difficult case (both difficult to the practical translator and a problem for linguistic theory of levels) of phonaesthetic meaning (contextual meaning of items less than morphemes) see "On Contextual Meaning", at n. 12, and the reference there to "On Comparative Descriptive Linguistics", p. 558, n. 2 (= Appendix G, n. 17).)

However, different levels require different criteria of comparison (kinds of *tertium quid comparationis*), both "extra-linguistic" (phonic (or graphic) substance or "context of stiuation") and intra-linguistic (formal or phonological (or graphological) meaning), the former being applicable at the two "ends" of the level scheme, in substance or phonology (or graphology) at one end, in context or form towards the other, the latter in form only and in phonology (or graphology) only.

[1] Halliday, "Categories", pp. 243–5; cf. n. 3 below.
[2] On F. R. Palmer's wish to go further and link levels when comparing languages see "Some Problems" (Appendix C), nn. 21, 32, 33.
[3] For Halliday, *op. cit.*, not only both primary levels and interlevels but grammar and lexis are all "levels"; another term still is needed to distinguish levels that are or contain demilevels (or levels and interlevels that contain or are alternative levels) and ones that are or do not. Cf. Appendix A.
[4] "On Contextual Meaning", at n. 14.

This distribution may be tabulated as follows:

phonic (or graphic) substance ⎱ criterion
phonology (or graphology)   ⎰ substantial ⎱ criterion intra-linguistic
form (grammar and lexis) ⎱ criterion ⎰ (formal/phonological meaning)
context[5]   ⎰ situational
                            (contextual meaning)

Little more need be said about the substantial or the phonic in general, which was treated with essential adequacy in W. S. Allen's seminal sketching of comparative descriptive linguistics.[6]

Phonology (or graphology) can be compared by two criteria (like form, see below), and should be compared inter alia by both in conjunction, e.g. partial identification of English initial "p" etc. and French initial "p" etc. on grounds not only of some substantial resemblance but (which as it were cancels out the substantial divergence as regards aspiration) the phonological opposition to "b" etc., if not to other series.

In the examples that follow (in 2.2) comparison will be at the level of form, but parallel examples, mutatis mutandis, could be taken from the other levels, e.g. from phonology.

These examples are moreover compared by the criterion of contextual meaning, but again comparison by the criterion of formal meaning is possible. The relation between the two, formal and contextual, calls for some discussion here.

In simple descriptive linguistics formal meaning (which in grammar is quantifiable) and formal criteria take logical precedence over contextual.[7]

In comparison, however, where the datum is not simply a

---

[5] Situation is omitted unlike substance because outside language in any sense (though a (primary) level of linguistic *analysis* (represented within language by context termed primary by Halliday "Categories", p. 243)), and therefore not (apart from possible statistics of instantial and thence potential situation-features) differing from language to language (what does differ being treatable under context). Context is included although not in fact susceptible of comparison independently of form.
[6] "Relationship in Comparative Linguistics", *Transactions of the Philological Society*, 1953, pp. 52–108 (pp. 88–100, especially 95–99).
[7] Halliday, "Categories", p. 245.

language understood as including its situation, or a pair or more of languages severally so understood (the subject-matter of application of descriptive theory to various languages, see below and cf. n. 18 on p. 24), but languages with some *tertium quid comparationis*, the relation of precedence between form and context is not the same.

Given two languages each with its formal meanings and then its contextual meanings already established in simple descriptive linguistics, comparison may be attempted of either formal or contextual or of both. As regards the formal, once given that what we are comparing is two (or more) languages, each susceptible to the methods of linguistic description, the form of each will fall into the categories of general linguistic theory, unit, structure, class, system, yielding formal meanings in the same kind of distribution (though the more delicate in each language (and cf. 2.21, n. 39), the more divergent from each other, and the more to compare in the sense of contrasting), e.g. clause having the formal meaning of exponence of element of structure of the sentence[8] and (in languages with equal number of units – so that the quantification of this instance of formal meaning indicates *formal* one-to-one correspondence (in abstraction from statistics of their exponence of structures)) of structure whose elements have as exponent the group.

However, comparison of formal meanings is ultimately dependent upon some identification other than formal, since this by definition is always intralinguistic, whereas contextual meaning relates to extralinguistic situation.[9] Such terminal points of the

[8]   There is an implication here that (whatever the total number of units) the highest and lowest unit (in grammar sentence and morpheme) may in any case be equated formally, as well as being termed identically – the identification and terminology of the intermediate ones, as part of the application of simple descriptive linguistic theory to different languages (cf. below), raises further problems, cf. Halliday, *LMT*, p. 150, on contextual criteria in such application (which is *not* the subject of the present work).

[9]   It might be argued that languages could be compared formally (or "phonologically") with otherwise, i.e. substantially and contextually, quite disparate complexes (systems or agglomerations of systems) such as games (as Saussure indeed compared "language", but not in detail, with chess), which would have to be from first to last purely in terms of the quantitative relations (and other logical relations) of the elements, and therefore *could* be compared so with other

formal framework as sentence, and language itself, are identifiable as corresponding only in relation to situation, and hence the other formal elements within the framework are identifiable ultimately so too. Thus the formal criterion is ultimately dependent on the contextual (though this certainly does not mean that the formal criterion is not operable at all).[10]

E.g. in comparing in two languages an utterance in each consisting of one or more sentence, the clauses of each may be put in correspondence according as they divide up the contextual meaning (cf. 2.21.2), provided that there is situational identity enabling one to equate contextual meaning, or (which may or may not give the same distribution) according as they correspond in formal meaning: say, least delicately, presupposition in dependence. But, though as clauses with contextual meaning and to be compared by it they are identified as clauses in each language by formal meaning, as clauses to be *compared* by formal meaning they are identified by formal relations which must include that to the higher unit, and ultimately to the utterance or to the whole language, where correspondence is through situation of utterance.

---

languages. To this it may be objected (as an argument relevant to comparative descriptive linguistics that has renewal of connection with natural languages) that not only does it remain to be demonstrated that any particular language would be found to resemble or differ from any non-language complex significantly more or less than any other particular language did (so that this kind of comparison had the effective delicacy to be relevant) but such abstract comparison being applied to the form or phonology (or graphology) of languages themselves without e.g. distinction of levels being rooted in situation of use might result in correspondences which had nothing to do with the real functioning of each language, or, more likely, in no correspondences of either real or illusory significance (in other words that the exponence-relation, between levels as well as within form and within phonology, is crucial to how language works as a whole). (The objection that languages and say games are of a quite different order of complexity could no doubt be met by postulating some kind of super-3-D-chess, and though the simulation of the open sets of lexis might prove difficult there, the wider fields of application of the Theory of Games such as economics could be invoked, but indeed it might be demonstrable by the mathematics of the Theory of Games that language, especially in its recursive structures, is decisively *sui generis* even in this limited sense, cf. the work on language and the mathematics of stochastic processes etc. by Chomsky, Bar-Hillel, and others.)

[10]   Cf. Huddleston, p. 294, Halliday, *LMT*, pp. 148, 150, 154.

However, one reason why the notion of the logical priority of the formal in linguistic comparison, though untenable, is tempting is that in *any* kind of linguistics the contextual seems not to be analysable and statable with the same rigour as the formal. To say this is in a sense to say nothing: the definition of form and context makes it tautologous; and to pursue formal-type rigour in the level of context, without introducing new scales of delicacy of analysis appropriate to contextual study,[11] would constitute a will o' the wisp of the most fatuous. Yet this needs saying, it needs pointing out most emphatically that the peculiar relation between comparative linguistics and the levels of situation and context, while making comparative linguistics possible at all, at the same time makes it of a different order (of rigour of demonstrability or what you will) from simple descriptive linguistics.[12]

This fact has been represented as entailing that "contextualization is a pseudo-procedure",[13] in the sense of D. Abercrombie's pseudo-procedures in linguistics.[14] Such a formulation is extreme; possible false conclusions from it need guarding against. If a pseudo-procedure is a procedure not able to be carried out in practice in all those cases where it might be appealed to in theory, then "contextualization" *is* a pseudo-procedure (possibly like a good many other procedures in linguistics[15]). But if a pseudo-procedure is an alleged procedure which because it cannot be carried out (either ever or in a given case) is of no help but is a positive hindrance in linguistics and therefore to be rejected from it, as Abercrombie's pseudo-procedures are,[16] then contextualization is *not* a pseudo-procedure.

[11] "On Contextual Meaning", at nn. 38–9.
[12] This is the element of truth in such critiques of "comparative linguistics" as Allen's in *RCL* (for other valuable aspects of which see *GLCP*, p. 164 ff. (Appendix B, p. 101 ff.), and *SPCL*, p. 58 (Appendix C, p. 120).
[13] Thomas and Barnes, "Contrastive Linguistics of Welsh and English", paper to Autumn Meeting of Linguistic Association (Great Britain), Bangor, 1963.
[14] D. Abercrombie, "Pseudo-procedures in Linguistics", *Zeitschrift für Phonetik, Sprachwissenschaft und Kommunikationsforschung*, 16 (1963), pp. 9–12.
[15] Cf. e.g. G. Meier's critique of minimal pairs, "Auf dem Wege zu einer kybernetischen Phonemtheorie", *ZfPSuK*, 16 (1963), pp. 327–335 (328).
[16] Even here there is surely a cline, e.g. Hockett's (*Course in Modern Linguistics*,

With these caveats, reference must be made for the principles of the process of contextualization in comparative linguistics to Halliday's critique in *Studies* pp. 64–5 of Allen's discussion in *RCL*, pp. 99–100, and to *GLCP*, p. 167 (= Appendix B, p. 104).

For practical purposes, in given instances of comparative descriptive linguistics and especially applied comparative descriptive linguistics, the problem of contextualization may be "solved" practically, while theoretically merely shifting it to another field of application, by utilizing texts and their translations already made (by "practical" translators, for some non-metalinguistic purpose) from the one language into the other. The assumption is made that the translation is "good", or adequate for the purpose of the linguistic comparison: for practical purposes this may be verified by the opinions of bilinguals; theoretically of course the verification would demand the whole process of "contextualization" over again.[17]

That this is so is, again a tautology, "because" the translator provides a situation common to the two languages only inasmuch as he proceeds from the *form*, with its potential contextual meanings mutually limiting each other to one or more possible instantial meanings,[18] of one language to (situation understood and from situation to be conveyed to) the *form*, with its contextual meanings ..., of the other language.[19] Situation of translator is (always in some way) distinct from situation of any original performer.[20]

So in the last resort translation, in this sense of published or other written or recorded texts (as distinct for example from "interpreting" in a live situation[21] with feedback,[22] with the observable

---

p. 323) counting of inter-idiolectal intelligibility (not included in published version of Abercrombie) responds more to our intuitions than does Ross's plotting of phonemes (Abercrombie, pp. 9–10). (Cf. Abercrombie, p. 9: "two sorts", though a different dividing-line.)

[17] See *OCDL*, especially p. 556, p. 565 (Appendix G, pp. 155, 169).

[18] See "On Contextual Meaning", at nn. 16–17.

[19] Cf. Catford, *op. cit.*

[20] Cf. Ure, *op. cit.*, e.g. p. 143(f).

[21] Here not the technical, comprehensive sense (cf. n. 30) but the technical "immediate situation" in its special application to literary utterance.

[22] Cf. Ure, *op. cit.*, pp. 138, 140.

indefinitely (and pseudo-procedurally?) adjustable by the linguistic researcher), provides only an approximation to "common situation" – for one thing something of the total "meaning" of the original will always be lost (whatever may be "gained") in the "meaning" of the form of the translation;[23] in this sense, admittedly a very delicate one relative to most purposes of linguistic comparison, translation from La into Lb and from La cannot be completely identified.

Many problems, then, remain to be solved in the part of general comparative linguistic theory relating comparative descriptive linguistics to the *levels* of general and descriptive linguistic theory and providing it with criteria of comparison: their solution can only be helped on (by "renewal of connection" with the data of languages under comparison) by utilizing the present provisional theoretical bases as fully as possible in concrete comparisons. At the same time, something needs to be said about other aspects of general and descriptive linguistic theory in relation to comparative linguistics.

For one, a clear distinction must be drawn between the comparative descriptive linguistics of languages and the application of simple descriptive linguistic theory to the description of languages severally (cf. n. 18 on p. 24). It is of course arguable that a. ultimately all languages may be describable in such terms that the description already contains the comparison,[24] b. in the meanwhile, description of any one language may be made (better "presented"[25]) for different purposes and if for comparative ones slanted accordingly (including language *under* description and language *of* description treated as a special case of languages *under comparison*), so that there is in fact a cline between description of a language in itself and comparison of it with another; but to establish a cline is not to obliterate the distinction between its ends.

A more particular point to be made concerns delicacy in comparison. All linguistic analysis is subject to a scale, or scales, of

[23]   Cf. *OCDL*, pp. 563–4 (Appendix G, pp. 167–68).
[24]   Cf. Halliday, *Studies*, p. 57, *LMT*, pp. 149, 154.
[25]   Halliday, "Categories", p. 246.

delicacy (scale of "depth of detail"[26]), of one sort or another. Comparison has its own scales of delicacy, expounded in 2.221. But *descriptive* delicacy itself, one of the scales essential to the demilevel of grammar,[27] enters into the data of comparison as much as the rest of the categorial framework of simple description (including the other scales of rank (e.g. (1.31) 2.21) and exponence (2.21 and n. 31)).

2.2 STEPS IN COMPARISON PROCESS

Descriptive linguistic comparison may be classified into ways of comparison, which are also possible stages in a comprehensive process of comparison, according as the languages under comparison are considered "instantially" along the chain or syntagmatic axis or "potentially" along the choice or paradigmatic axis.[28] In the latter case one is comparing systems and the occurrence of their members (classes) in structures ("systemic comparison"), in the former the realization of structures, and of choices within systems. in texts of longer or shorter extent ("linear or textual comparison"). Each kind complements the other, and the process in which they are stages is in a sense circular (or spiral) (see 2.2221), but it is to say the least (cf. 2.22 *init.*) convenient to begin with the linear or textual.

2.21 *Linear-Textual Comparison (with Rank-bound Translation)*

Here one is comparing concrete samples of given languages in their specific correspondence to each other (for generalization from them *as* samples, see 2.2221), which implies (for most purposes at least) restriction to the criterion of situation and therefore the level of form (comparison of substantially comparable utterances would be restricted to very short ones and in principle trivial (though cf.

---

[26] Halliday, "Categories", pp. 258–9.
[27] Halliday, "Categories", pp. 268–273.
[28] Rank-bound translation is a special case, if it *is* considered to be comparison properly speaking, being a statement about parts of a text in one language in terms of potential occurrences in the other.

Catford on "double"/"deux boules" as a complete utterance[29]), and comparison of text with comparable formal meaning would presuppose both situational comparability (cf. 2.1) and systemic comparison). This involves in each case an identifiable situation (in the comprehensive sense[30]) and the utterance or text in each language correlating with it. For practical purposes, as was argued in 2.1, translations will be assumed to provide this (though with the proviso there that theoretically the problem is only pushed back to that of justifying the practical translator).

For present purposes it will be assumed that either language a translated into language b or language b translated into language a can be regarded as languages a and b in correspondence. (La → Lb/Lb → La = La:Lb, where the sequence ab is arbitrary.) Refinement on this would pertain in the first instance to translation theory (cf. 1.31) and then to the feedback of translation theory to comparative descriptive linguistics (2,1, 1.31). One must distinguish the one-way relation of 2.2223, occurring more generally than in translation.

The actual process of comparison begins when full description of each text, representing understanding of text and knowledge of systems, etc., involved, is already achieved. For practical purposes of exposition to an audience without some of this for at least one of the texts, use may be made of rank-bound translation (see 1.31), which is therefore included here (as 0.) before the stages (1. -) of linear comparison proper, although (cf. n. 28) it is not comparison of text with text, nor of systems, thus in a sense not *comparison* at all (but glossing of items, analysis of text).[31]

Example of linear or textual comparison:[32]

[29]   Graphic is also possible, e.g. *Шур* handwritten read as "Uljyp". But cf. Halliday, *LMT*, p. 148.
[30]   I.e. including wider situation and especially thesis as well as immediate situation.
[31]   It might be considered to be comparison of relations between exponence of ranks in given cases in two languages, the relation in the one in the given case being identity.
[32]   *Thérèse*, p. 260, 1.17; F. Mauriac, *La Fin de la Nuit* (1935) (Paris, Grasset, 1947), p. 158, 1.19: text and analysis of clause and verbal group structure of the French from Huddleston, p. 296 (cf. nn. 17–18 on p. 24).

|| elle ne se posait | pas | la question || P(snav)AC
|| she | did not ask | herself | the question || SPCC[33]

2.210 *Rank-bound Translation*

Rank-bound translation (symbolization a → B, b → A, where a, b = texts, A, B = languages).

a. English → French

M	X X X demander X X X question
W	elle X X demander elle-même X question
G	elle n'a *etc.* pas demandé *etc.* se la question
C	elle ne s'est pas posé la question
T	elle ne se posait pas la question

b. French → English

M	X X X put X X X question
W	she X X put X X question
G	she did not put herself not the (·624[34]) question
C	she did not ask herself the question (C ·516)

2.211 *One-way (linear) Comparative Statement* (symbolization: $a \rightarrow b, b \rightarrow a$)

This, like the rank-bound translation, begins from the one text ("source language") and its elements of structure ("a"/"b"), but now the item of the other language put in correspondence with each is not, as in rank-bound translation, the most likely in the language in general ("B"/"A") but that in the actual text ("b"/"a") in the other language ("target language"), specifically the item there which would be altered if that in the first were altered; there may in fact be more than one item in either language linked in this way, as liable to alternation together, and this is indicated as necessary by repeating them with a linking index number.[35] In this example

---

[33] P = predicator, A = adjunct, C = complement, S = subject, in English and French: these are elements of the structure of the clause (cf. 1.31, n. 19); s = subject, n = negative, a = adjunct, v = verb: elements of the structure of the French verbal group.

[34] See p. 50.

[35] Here of course all morphemes and other units, including grammatical items, are "translated"; morpheme cuts are sometimes crude (cf. n. 19 on p. 24), and would be better, but less concisely, represented by categorial formulations, e.g. di- and -d by "stem-morpheme" and "past tense morpheme" "*of did*".

there is no need for statement above the group, since clause etc. are in obvious one-to-one correspondence; and for the same general reason of divergence increasing *down* the rank scale, the order is reversed as compared with rank-bound translation (cf. 1.31 (n. 14)).

a. English → French

	she	did	not	ask	herself	the	question
G	elle - t | ne		posai - pas		|se	| la	question
W	elle - t | ne .. pas 1	-ai- | ne .. pas 2 | pos - | se			| 1 | a question
M	elle 1 - t | ne .. pas 1 | -ai- | ne .. pas 2 | pos - | elle 2 | se |			1 | a question

b. French → English

	elle	ne	se	posait	pas	la	question
G	| she did not 1 ask herself				| di-not 2 | the		question
W	| she 1 | di-not 1 | herself | ask	-d	she 2 | di-not 2 | the | question
M	| she 1 | di-not 1 | herself | ask | -d | she 2 | di-not 2 | the | question

The statement can and in a complete account should also be made of the categories (in terms of structure) at each degree of delicacy (of the first language[36]), of which the formal items are the ultimate formal exponents, e.g.

English (first degree) → French

	S (h)[37]	P	C (h)	C (mh)
G	| (P)s ... (v) 1 |	P(nv(2)) A	| (P)a |	C
W	| (P)s ... (v) 1 | n ... A 1(v) 2 | n ... A2 | (v)3 | (P)a | (β) 1 | α (β) 2

2.212 *Equal (-linear) Comparative Statement* (symbolization: $a:b$).[38]

In 2.211 the statement is determined by one language or the other as to the framework of elements of structure from which it begins. A statement equal for both languages in this respect is obtained at cost of leaving behind the structure "in itself" of each language, by gathering up the minimum components of correspondence in 2.211 (a. and b.) and listing them; the sequence of listing may be determined arbitrarily as following the linear/textual

[36] Cf. 2.1 on comparison of delicacies, and n. 39 below.
[37] Elements of structure of nominal group: English h = head, m = modifier (pre-head); French α = presupposed, β = presupposing. (Cf. 1.31, n. 19.) For the brackets in the French see below, 2.212 *ad fin.*
[38] For an extended example of this stage, as regards formal items, see "On Comparative Descriptive Linguistics".

sequence of one language ("a.") or the other ("b.") (an alphabetical sequence, for example, would look "more equal" (though still according to one language) but, even with numerical indices, show the sequence of either text less graphically), but this does not affect the equality of item-correspondence (abstracting from sequence as exponent of formal meanings, or indicating it by numerical indices where necessary).

(following English sequence)

i	she . . . her- (6)	:	elle . . . -t (6)
ii	di- . . . not (4)	:	ne . . . pas (7)
iii	-d	:	-ai- (5)
iv	ask (5)	:	pos- (4)
v	-self (7)	:	se (3)
vi	the (8)	:	1– (8)
vii	question (9)	:	-a question (9)

Following French sequence would change v to after ii and reverse iii and iv. Alphabetically (according to English):

i	ask 5	:	pos- 4
ii	-d 3	:	-ai- 5
iii	di- 2 . . . not 4	:	ne 2 . . . pas 7
iv	question 9	:	-a question 9
v	-self 7	:	se 3
vi	she 1 . . . her- 6	:	elle 1 . . . -t 6
vii	the 8	:	1- 8

Again the statement can and should be made also of the elements of structure[39] of which the formal items are the exponents,[40] e.g., primary degree of delicacy,[41] (with ( ) indicating unit in structure

---

[39] If beyond primary degree of delicacy, the choice will be arbitrary, secondary degrees in both languages having no fixed comparability; cf. above at n. 36, and 2.1, and below, 2.3.

[40] That the "bits" in correspondence always are formal items expounding units of each language (if "only", as most often, morphemes) follows from the principle mentioned above (2.1, 2.21) of translation-situation having its correlation in *form*; cf. "On Comparative Descriptive Linguistics", p. 560 (Appendix G, p. 157).

[41] Cf. n. 39.

of which the given item expounds an element): –

(α element of sentence structure:[42] α)

i	S . . . ((C)h)	: (P) s . . . (v)
ii	(P)	: (P) n . . . A
iii	,,	: ((P) v\
iv	,,	: ,,
v	((C) h)	: (P) a
vi	(C) m	: (β)
vii	(C) h	: (C) (β) α

2.22 *Systemic Comparison*

By "systemic" here is not meant necessarily the strict sense of the term "system"[43] in the theory of grammar and phonology, where closed systems (of classes) occur at places in structure. As explained in 2.2, the opposition is between linear or syntagmatic, in 2.21, and paradigmatic, here, and the latter may include lexical sets or other groupings or "sets" of grammatical items or categories not necessarily forming systems (e.g. primary elements of clause-structure) – this is particularly true of 2.2221 (cf. on delicacy of extent of system below). The term "systemic" here however partly derives from, and can certainly be justified by, Allen's dictum[44] that "[descriptive] comparison is of systems not languages".

As was said above, neither linear/textual nor "systemic" comparison can lay claim to complete logical precedence, but convenience of exposition is certainly served by disposing of linear/textual before embarking on "systemic". In fact, the data of generalization of linear correspondences (see 2.2221) derive from linear/textual, although at the same time the data of rank-bound translation should be derived from generalization of linear correspondences (see 2.2221 *ad fin.*).

In its turn generalization of linear correspondences provides

---

[42]   Cf. 2.1, circa nn. 8–10. The relation of presupposition in dependence of any elements (cf. n. 37) is represented by β to α.
[43]   Halliday, "Categories", pp. 264–5.
[44]   W. S. Allen, *RCL*, pp. 53, 87.

data for equal-systemic (2.2222) and one-way systemic comparison (2.2223).

These relations form a network which can be symbolized thus (→ means "proceeding from one stage to the other"): [45]

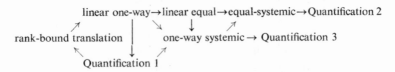

Of this diagram a part of significance for the relation of 2.21 and 2.22, namely "[linear(one-way → equal) → one-way systemic] → equal-systemic",[45] can be expanded (anticipating the exemplifications in 2.2223 and 2 (and 1)) as follows: –

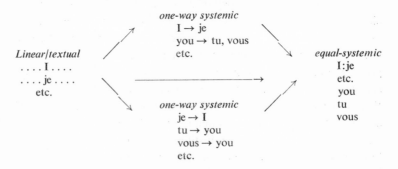

It will be observed that the relation between the "equal" and "one-way" divisions of linear and of systemic is hardly symmetrical, and only economy of terminology may justify the parallelism of name. In linear one-way is merely a step, included for completeness of exposition, in proceeding from the framework of each language, as illustrated in rank-bound translation, to a complete comparative textual statement equally oriented to the frameworks of both languages. (This sense of one-way could be symbolized specifically

[45] On the relative merits of two-dimensional and linear formulations cf. Y. R. Chao, "Graphic and Phonetic Aspects of Linguistic and Mathematical Symbols", *Proceedings of the 12th Symposium in Applied Mathematics* (*Structure of Language and its Mathematical Aspects*) (Providence, 1961), pp. 69–82 (p. 72).

as $-L\rightarrow$ (L for linear), and that in rank-bound translation as $-TP\rightarrow$ (TP for translation probability).) The difference between equal and one-way in systemic is more fundamental, as will be seen in 2.2222 and 2.2223. (Symbolized specifically as $-S\rightarrow$, or $-TA\rightarrow$ (TA for translation alternatives).)

In a more trivial sense still than in linear/textual comparison, the one-way concept also enters into (2.2221) generalization of linear correspondences, which will be stated either for La in relation to Lb or for Lb in relation to La, e.g. in the example given in 2.2221 the statement is for French in relation to English, i.e. proportions of occurrences of the French item with particular English correspondences. This one-way relation (symbolized specifically as $-Q\rightarrow$ (Q for quantification), e.g. French $-Q\rightarrow$ English) is of course independent of which language (text) is the translation of the other (cf. 2.1, 2.21, 2.2223) and indeed can apply equally to two languages both translating a third not under comparison[46] (the ("practical") translation-relation being symbolized specifically as $-T\rightarrow$, e.g. a $\leftarrow T-$ c $-T\rightarrow$ b (then A $-Q\rightarrow$ B/B $-Q\rightarrow$ A)).

The final and lengthiest (2.221) topic to be disposed of before proceeding to the kinds of systemic comparison themselves is that of the scales of delicacy of comparison. These did not need to be mentioned before discussing linear/textual comparison, since in comparing texts themselves, delicacy of extent of text or of frequency of item (delicacy no. 3) does not arise, as it does in the generalization of linear correspondences, delicacy of co-textual or situational environment (delicacy no. 2) is (if co-textual) or (if situational) is assumed (cf. 2.1) complete, and delicacy of extent of system compared (delicacy no. 1) most of all presupposes systemic not linear comparison. (The same irrelevance to linear (again as distinct from generalization of linear correspondences) applies to quantification, dealt with under each kind of systemic comparison (2.2221-3).)

---

[46] A familiar example would be bible translations (a $\leftarrow T-$ Greek (or English, etc.) $-T\rightarrow$ b), with Greek (or English, etc.) entering not into the immediate comparison process but at most into some auxiliary procedure such as verifying the contextual meaning.

2.221 *Scales of Delicacy of Comparison*

Delicacy is depth of detail[47] of analysis or of other linguistic operation.[48] In addition to general and descriptive delicacy entering into comparison (see 2.1), comparative descriptive linguistics has its own *delicacy of comparison*.

Of this three scales may be distinguished, according as variation is in the system under comparison, in the environment considered of the item under comparison, or in the text and with it the number of occurrences of a given item.

These apply to grammar or (with set etc. for system etc.) lexis, but not (altogether) equally to the kinds of systemic comparison. The discussion below will assume application to grammar.

2.2211 *Delicacy of Extent of System.*

– This may be a question either, in recursive structures, of the degree of depth to which the comparison is taken,[49] or, in grammatical systems generally, of degrees of distinction of more restricted classes, e.g. of lexical items associated with the system in question (e.g. *I'm going*, but *I think*, sometimes *I'm thinking*).

This scale enters into equal-systemic (2.2222) and one-way systemic (2.2223) comparison, but not as such into generalization of linear correspondences (2.2221) of individual items, though any bringing together or arranging of (results for) different items will imply a selection of "systems". Equal-systemic and one-way systemic themselves may be distinguished by the possible degree of abstraction of systems from exponents (see 2.2223).

2.2212 *Delicacy of Differentiation of Environment.*

– The environment differentiated may be either co-textual (e.g. Czech *vy jste znal(i)* (or Russian вы ласкавый/е)) or situational (e.g. Russian вы знали (or Czech *vy znáte*) addressing one or more).[50]

---

[47]   Halliday, "Categories", p. 272. Cf. 2.1 above.
[48]   Cf. "Possible Comparisons", pp. 297–8 (Appendix F, pp. 150–52); "On Contextual Meaning".
[49]   See "Possible Comparisons", p. 298 (Appendix F, p. 151).
[50]   Cf. "Possible Comparisons", pp. 297–8 (Appendix F, p. 151).

This scale enters into all three kinds of systemic comparison, e.g. in the generalization of linear correspondences the example given in 2.2221 has variation of this delicacy between the simple item *dans* and this item in environment, or complex item,[51] motion-verb – *dans* – place-noun.

2.2213 *Delicacy of Extent of Text/Frequency of Item.* – In general, the more text compared the more delicate the comparison. In particular (and whether this coincides with the general depends on the text, i.e. on relative frequency within it), the more occurences of a particular item in the text compared, the more delicate the comparison of that item (e.g. the greater scope for delicacy of differentiation of environment).

This scale enters immediately into generalization of linear correspondences, and with the data from that into equal-systemic and one-way systemic comparison (especially if weighting is to be introduced into these (cf. 2.3)).

2.222 *Kinds of Systemic Comparison*

As was said above (2.22) these are classed together as being essentially paradigmatic or generalizing rather than linear or textual; in particular, the scales of delicacy of comparison apply in some measure to them all, including that most apparently bound to prior textual analysis, generalization of linear correspondences (2.2221).

The order followed in their exposition rests upon the considerations, firstly that generalization of linear correspondences furnishes the other two with evidence for their identifications, secondly that of the other two equal-systemic was prior in its historical origination (cf. nn. 54 and 69) and may be treated as prior in the logic of the exposition (despite the relations in the logic of the process itself exhibited in the diagram in 2.22).

[51] This formulation may suggest an indistinct borderline with delicacy of extent of system; the distinction is essentially between the point of view of *syntagmatic* environment (or environment of *instantial* situation) and the *paradigmatic* point of view. (Cf. Halliday, *LMT*, p. 148 ("either in sequence or in combination").)

2.2221 *Generalization of Linear Correspondences* symbolization: $a{:}b \rightarrow A{:}B \ (A-Q\rightarrow B/B-Q\rightarrow A)$. – The *linear correspondences* established by linear/textual comparison are generalized by taking those for a given item in one language, in a certain corpus of text, and stating the proportions of them in which given items occur in the other language. For example, an instance quoted by Catford,[52] in 12,000 words of French in translation-correspondence with English, of 134 occurrences of *dans* 73% corresponded to *in* ($dans-Q\rightarrow in = \cdot73$); 19% to *into*; when *dans* was preceded by a verb of motion and followed by a noun of place the correspondence with *into* approximated 100%.

The probabilities obtained in this way (and specifically the majority correspondence) provide an objective source (of varying precision according to the scales of delicacy of comparison, and to similarity of register (cf. 1.34) chosen) for the data of rank-bound translation. For example, in 1.31 and 2.21, the figures given with certain translations, such as "the carrots" as subject, "the question" as complement, are the proportions found by Huddleston, *op. cit.*, in the texts he used, of occurrence of French items with the given translation: English subject translating French subject; English extensive complement translating French extensive complement.

A further example (Polish → English[53]) will illustrate majority translation at different ranks:

```
        Czy     pan  go      zna?
M    X gentleman X X know X (imperfective → X (present---present = ·75)
                             non-continuous = ·94)
W    whether ,, him knows (present imperfective → present non-continuous = ·8)
(S    Do you know him?)
```

---

[52] in *A Linguistic Theory of Translation*. Altogether, a considerable amount of such work has been done, and valuable statistical samples for various languages accumulated, under Catford's general direction at the Edinburgh School of Applied Linguistics.
[53] Texts and statistics from H. Ulatowska, "A Comparison of Verb Forms in Polish and English in the Language of Medical Science and Fiction respectively . . .", Edinburgh Diploma in Applied Linguistics dissertation (unpub.), 1959. Similar results for Russian are not yet available.

Poviem panu co zrobię.

M X^1 (*perfective* → say X^2 (*present* → X gentleman X X X^1 do X^2 X
      non-continuous = ·99 *present* = ·75)

W I('ll) say (*present perfective* → *will*/to the g. what I('ll) do
      shall non-continuous = ·46
      present   „   = ·46)

S I tell you what I'll do.

In this example, while Polish –Q→ and –TP→ English (see 2.22), in the texts from which the sentences and statistics come (sentences from E. Waugh's *Scoop* and its translation *Dziennikarz z przypadku*) Polish ←T– English; on the irrelevance of this to directions of comparison cf. 2.1, 2.21, 2.2223.

A reverse example, using the same source of statistics but the sentence of 1.21 –

I   have   come.

M X mie- X (*present* → *present* = ·87 X przychodzi- X (→ *imperfective* X
      non-continuous → *imperfective* = ·6)   = ·6

W ja   mam etc. („   „   )   „
G (ja)   przychodził- (*present perfect non-continuous* → *imperfective*
                                past = ·41 (majority))
(C (ja) przychodziłem)
S Przyszedłem.

2.2222 *Equal-systemic Comparison (symbolization: A(Sa): B(Sb)* (where S = "system")). Valuable as the findings of generalization of linear comparison are, in themselves and for such purposes as rank-bound translation, they are but raw material in relation to the other kinds of "systemic" comparison themselves. The generalize comparison further by confronting comparable systems, which in its turn may be developed into larger-scale comparison of languages (2.3).

The comparison of linguistic items as terms in systems, and the methods originated for this by W. S. Allen,[54] have been treated and developed[55] elsewhere.[56] The steps involved may be summar-

[54] *RCL*, pp. 90–2, 94–100.
[55] To Allen's treatment have been added: extension of contextualization (and elaboration of criteria generally, see 2.1) and hence of systems comparable; *delicacy* of comparison (and possible weighting); modification of the mathematical formula.
[56] *GLCP* (= Appendix B), Halliday in *Studies*, *SPCL* (= Appendix C), "Possible Comparisons" (=Appendix F), Levenston and Ellis (n. 69 below).

ized as: establishment of systems as (sufficiently) comparable and
their terms as (partly) identifiable (cf. 2.1),[57] with specification of
delicacies of comparison (2.221) conditioning relative degrees of
identification (2.221 and 2.2221; for possible weighting see below);
reduction of the two systems to a "generic system" ("AB" (Allen) /
Sab) consisting of the terms in one-to-one correspondence (at
given degrees of delicacy) plus the remaining terms in each system,
as distinct from the "aggregate system" or simple sum of the numbers of terms in the two systems together; statement (at the given
degrees of delicacy) of the extent of correspondence of the systems,
i.e. the proportion of terms identifiable with each other (as corresponding one-to-one) at the given degrees of delicacy; finally
quantification of this, as a value between 0 and 1,[58] the formula
here used[59] being "degree of correspondence $= \frac{c}{g}$", where $c =$
number of terms in one-to-one correspondence (e.g. $I{:}je$), $g =$
generic system, i.e. $c + n{-}c$ (number of terms not in one-to-one
correspondence, e.g. *you*, *tu*, *vous*). With this specific quantitative
conclusion the method as a whole may be termed "system-reduction method" of descriptive comparison of languages and quantification thereof.

The method may be further extended by the introduction of
weighting of the values of terms in correspondence according to the
frequency of the given correspondence in the texts providing the
degree of delicacy of extent of text, either as a straight magnitude
(e.g. 53%, 30%, 17% as 53, 30, 17) or using cut-offs additional to
the simple majority basis of identification in the non-weighted use
of frequency data (e.g. – with cut-offs at 50% and 20% – 53%,
30%, 17% as 2, 1, 0).

The "system-reduction" method is not of course the only possible
way of quantifying equal-systemic comparison, and indeed in
particular cases may be less suitable. For example, the numerals
lend themselves more directly to another procedure, and though

[57] "Possible Comparisons" (Appendix F), n. 48.
[58] *RCL*, p. 92, "Possible Comparisons", pp. 296–7, 298–9 (Appendix F, pp.
149–50, 152–3), Levenston and Ellis.
[59] *PCBNWELC*, pp. 296–7, 298 with n. 52 (Appendix F, pp. 149–50, 152).

this could be converted (keeping the criterion formal) into the system-reduction formula for extent of correspondence (by treating *this* index of correspondence as the "generic system" (see below)), and indeed would have to be if its content were to be brought into the same process of "metacomparison" with other parts of the languages (see 2.3), for other purposes it will suffice unconverted.[60]

Numbers, as expounded in any language by "numeral(word)s", do not form a closed system, arithmetical numbers being the proto-typical open set; but the numeral morphemes and further (recursive) components composing their exponents do (though not necessarily in the strict sense of grammatical system (cf. 2.22, *init.*)). Moreover, if the ordinary system-reduction procedure with contextual criterion[61] were to be applied to the numeral words, there would be complete correspondence, the generic "system" for the two languages and the "system" of either language being identical.

What does differ from language to language is the structure of the higher numerals (i.e. the more-than-one-morpheme structure of numeral words expounding higher numbers).[62] The extent to which this differs between any two languages can be quantified (scil. in inverse proportion to the extent of correspondence, which is the reverse of the system-reduction formula) by stating the minimum number of equivalences, of elements or structures, ne-

[60] This particular alternative to the usual "system-reduction method" (it does in fact embody a kind of reduction of systems (to a generic system), the first step in the usual method) is convenient for numerals because there the size of the aggregate, as distinct from the generic, system, seems not to be in the same need of specification for distinctive comparison.

[61] Identical formal items (identical with certain numeral forms) may have (expound lexical formal meaning corresponding to) non-(definite)numerical contextual meaning, e.g. Turkish *kırk* (40), "umpteen", colloquial contemporary English *fifty-seven*, French *trente-six* (cf. German *sieben Sachen*, etc.), Greek μυριάς, Russian тьма, older Rumanian *întuneric*, Chinese *wàn* (10,000), "countless". This is here excluded on the delicacy scales of extent of system and possibly of contextual environment or of frequency.

[62] This implies further a different *contextual* meaning for some components, e.g. Chinese component *shí* (entering into e.g. *shí yí*, 11, *shí sì*, 14, *liù shí*, 60, *shí wàn*, 100,000, as well as *shí*, 10) would have a different contextual meaning from English *ten* (beside *eleven, fourteen, sixty, a hundred thousand*), but in fact (once given the contextual correspondence of all the numeral words) comparison can be simply of form. (Cf. also n. 63.)

cessary to form all possible (cardinal) numerals in both (termed here the "(two-language) numeral index"). (It is of course also possible to state the minimum number of elements and structures necessary for each language (termed here the "single-language index"), which will give a *lower limit* for the minimum for the two languages (numeral index), but to complete this requires the actual correspondences between them; it is also possible to adapt this to one-way comparison, see 2.2223.)

For example, to take two languages with relatively simple inventories (Chinese itself in fact approaches the minimum single-language index for a decimal system with morphemes for powers of ten up to 10,000[63]), Chinese and Turkish:[64]

Both languages have for 1–19 ten components (1–10),[65] and one

---

[63]   Cf. Chao, *op. cit.* (2.22, n. 45, above), p. 75: "Symbols and symbol complexes. Here a distinction should be drawn between (1) the arbitrariness of symbol to its denotatum and (2) the presence or absence of systematic relation between symbols and their denotata. The very nature of symbolism consists in the arbitrariness of association, and it is of no particular advantage that Chinese characters are written one, two, and three strokes for the numbers one, two, and three, especially as that is given up from four on. On the other hand it is of definite advantage symbol-wise that the numbers 11, 12 . . . 20, 21 . . . 30 . . . are called ten-one, ten-two, . . . two-ten, two-ten-one, . . . three-ten, etc., as against the German order, which does not correspond to the graphic symbols. It is true that before adopting such a way of saying the numbers, it ought to be shown that it is unique and consistent. But the ancient Chinese apparently found that out when they used the scheme and met with no difficulty in practical applications for several thousand years." Correspondence to graphic symbols (including figures) is of course not directly relevant to our present purpose (any more than the difference between Chinese morphemic writing into which Chinese figures fit (as mostly identical with characters for numeral components) and German (predominantly) alphabetical writing which differentiates figures and spelling out of numerals), but German numeral (component)s between 12 and 100 (except the tens) do not only exhibit sequence different from the figures but different from those above 100, e.g. *zweitausend dreihundert fünfundachtzig.* 2(i)3(ii)8(iv)5(iii).
[64]   These are also convenient examples in having (almost) no such forms as English *forty* beside *four* which would make the index different for the written and the spoken language – the one exception is the place of the accent in Turkish, *ón iki* (12) and *yirmí iki* (22) having identical structure in writing, *on iki, yirmi iki*: the index given below is the higher one, for the spoken language.
[65]   Chinese: *yī, èr* (or *liǎng*, this alternation being an independent system of numeral in nominal group), *sān, sì, wǔ, liù, qī, bā, jiǔ, shí*; Turkish: *bir, iki, üç, dört, beş, altı, yedi, sekiz, dokuz, on.*

structure, for 11–19 (*shí èr*,[66] *on iki* (see n. 64), 12, etc.); for 20–99, eight more components (20–90,[67] the structure of the Chinese (*èr shí*, 20, etc.) being irrelevant to the two-language numeral index, since the Turkish are irreducible) and two structures (*èr shí yī*, *yirmi bir* (see n. 64), 21, etc.); for 100 upwards four more components (100, 1000, 10,000 (Chinese irreducible), 1,000,000 (Turkish irreducible[68])) and the same structures plus exceptional ones for 100 (Chinese *yìbăi* beside Turkish *yüz*), for teens within higher numbers (Chinese – *yìshí* (–) beside Turkish – *on* (–)), for one thousand do. (Chinese – *yìqiān* (–) beside Turkish – *bin* (–)), for 10,000 (Chinese *yíwàn* beside Turkish *on bin*), and for 2,000 and 20,000 (Chinese *liăngqiān* and *liăngwàn* beside 20, *èrshí*, 200, *èrbăi*) (e.g. 26,357,418, *èr qiān liù băi shí wŭ wàn qī qiān sì băi, yīshí bā, yirmi alti milyon üç yüz elli yedi bin dört yüz ón sekiz*): in all, twenty-two (primary) components and eight structures, = (numeral index:) 30 (as compared with single-language indices, Chinese = 20, Turkish = 24).

The numeral index could be converted, if necessary (see above), into the system-reduction formula by treating the system in each language as consisting of the number of terms in the single-language index for that language, the aggregate system then being the two single-language indices combined, and the generic system as being the numeral index, the number of correspondents being the aggregate minus the generic. Thus the value for our example would be $\frac{20+24-30}{30} = \frac{14}{30} = .47$. (Note that the value 0 could only result from the impossible situation of numeral index made up of single-language indices without any overlap at all.)

2.2223 *One-way Systemic Comparison* (symbolization: *A(Sa)* → *B* (*Sb*), *B(Sb)* → *A(Sa)* (*–S→/–TA→*)). – This extension (keeping delicacies, etc.) of system-reduction method, beyond equal-systemic

[66] The Chinese transcription is into the new official Roman orthography.
[67] Chinese: *èr shí*, etc.; Turkish *yirmi, otuz, kırk, elli, altmış, yetmiş, seksen, doksan*, Turkish *altmış* and *yetmiş* (beside *altı*, 6, and *yedi*, 7) and even *seksen* and *doksan* (beside *sekiz*, 8, and *dokuz*, 9) being treated each as two items.
[68] Chinese: *băi, qiān, wàn, băi wàn*; Turkish: *yüz, bin, on bin, milyon*.

statement, was originally devised[69] in order to apply descriptive linguistic comparison to concrete purposes for which equal-systemic statement appeared ill-fitted, namely the applied linguistics of language teaching, of "practical" translation (cf. 1.31, 2.1) and of other forms of proceeding *from* one language *to* another, where the question of relative ease of transition in the two directions between a pair of languages, as regards a given feature or system, demands a formulation that distinguishes the two directions.

This is achieved by replacing "c" in the equal-systemic formula (2.2222) by the number of $1(+) \rightarrow 1$ ($-TA\rightarrow$) correspondences (e.g. $I \rightarrow je$), and "n–c" by the number of $1 \rightarrow 1+$ correspondences (e.g. *you* → a. *tu*, b. *vous*).

For the particular purposes of this method, it may be appropriate to start out from discrete exponents, e.g. *he, she, it, they*, with less abstraction of systems, e.g. person-number separated from gender, than for equal-systemic. Another difference is the value of "0" (cf. 2.3).

Again, and possibly with more widespread application than in equal-systemic comparison, *weighting* is possible (cf. 2.3).

It should be noted that the relation $-TA\rightarrow$ is independent of the relation $-T\rightarrow$ (see 2.22) in the texts used for proportion of correspondences (cf. 2.1, 2.21, 2.2221). I.e. "translation-alternative" refers to correspondences for any purpose of transition from the one language to the other, "practical translation" being only one of these.

In the same general way, a one-way comparison can be made of "numeral indices" (see 2.2222 ad fin.).

Chinese → Turkish: $1(+) \rightarrow 1$: 1–10, 100 (as component), 1000, 10,000 (as component), 100, 10,000: total 15.
structures with *yìshí* and *yìgiān* and for 2,000 and 20,000: 3 total 18
$1 \rightarrow 1+$: structure "(powers of) ten(s) + unit" → a. 11–19, b. above 20: 2
structure "unit x (powers of) ten" → a.-h. 20–90, i. 1,000,000, j. others: 10   total 12.

---

[69]   See E. Levenston and J. Ellis, "A Transfer Grammar Development of System-Reduction Quantification Method", *Zeitschrift für Phonetik*, 17 (1964), pp. 449–452.

$$\frac{c}{c + n\text{-}c} = \frac{8}{30}$$

Turkish → Chinese: 1(+)→ 1: 1–10, 20–90, 100, 1000, 1,000,000, structure
11–19:total 21
1 → 1+: structure "unit X powers of ten" →
a. 10,000 (as component), b. 100, c. 10,000, d. 2,000 and
20,000, e. others: total 5
structure "(powers of) tens + lower components"→ a. teens
within higher numbers, b. one thousand do., c. rest: total 3

$$\frac{c}{c + n\text{-}c} = \frac{21}{29}$$

2.3 COMPARISON OF COMPARISONS

Comparison of comparisons or "metacomparison" brings together many of the threads of comparative linguistics, into a nexus from which new lines of development of the subject may radiate.

In talking of "metacomparative" work it is not intended here to refer to (comparative) study of approaches to linguistic comparison, of theories (cf. Introduction, and 2.1), models (cf. 2.1), procedures, or methods (cf. 2.2, 2.22), as "metalanguage" or (the non-Whorfian sense of) "metalinguistic" does to discourse about language or linguistics (or what might be called "comparative linguistic theory" or less ambiguously "comparative general linguistics"). But as metalanguage or metalinguistic discourse is "language turned back on itself",[70] so metacomparison is (the abstract process, quantifiable, of) comparison "turned back on" (primary linguistic) comparisons.

The distinction, as suggested in 1.1, is important, between the primary comparison of the language data themselves and the (meta)comparative operations performable on them (the primary results) and on the results of these operations themselves recursively. While maintaining and developing the former as the channel for "renewal of connection", the latter call for developing as providing the power of mathematical generality in condensing and summing up the results of various kinds of comparative linguistics.

[70] Cf. *GLCP*, n. 103 (Appendix B, n. 102).

Aside from the various approaches to quantification of comparative linguistics that in effect combine primary comparison and metacomparison, referred to in 1.1, and for example in n. 4, suggestions for metacomparing the basic quantitative aspects of *particular descriptive* comparison (outlined in 2.22) already made are (for 2.2222) "a formula giving figures ranging from 0 to a potential ∞" in order "to state an *extent* of relationship, in so far as the *number* of systems included in the comparison, as well as the overall reduction of categories, is also an important index of the systemization",[71] and "further statistical operations" "called for if and when individual values for individual systems and (relevant parts of) individual pairs of languages are accumulated, in order to give values for sets of systems and of languages and summations of values for pairs and sets of languages and of summations in 'metacomparison' ... adding the fractional (between 0 and 1) values, and stating the total as for, or divided by, the number of systems, etc., in question",[72] and (for 2.2223) "the same ... in general ... for systems ... but ... additions involving 0 as 'numerator' ["In the one-way method, when the 'numerator' is 0, the 'denominator' remains none the less significant of the degree of difficulty of transition (as compared with other pairs with 'numerator' 0), and the process cannot be treated as a mathematical division, but must be stated with the 'denominator' retained."] could not proceed in a normal mathematical way; and there seems no way of making additions for languages ... problems might possibly be solved by some alternative procedure of mathematical formulation from the start",[73] thus a case of metacomparison reacting back on primary comparison quantification methods.

With all of these, weighting for frequency (relating 2.2222–3 to 2.2221) also comes into question. Even this however would appear able only partly to solve the problems in metacomparison raised

---

[71]   W. S. Allen, *RCL*, p. 93. By "relationship" here is apparently meant, as elsewhere in *RCL*, correspondence of systems (irrespective of genetic significance).
[72]   Ellis, "Possible Comparisons", p. 299 (Appendix F, pp. 152-3).
[73]   Levenston and Ellis, *op. cit.*

by the present "unmeasurability" of (grammatical) delicacy.[74] An example to illustrate this is given below under application to areal convergence.

But as ever the techniques of particular comparative descriptive linguistics (.211) will underlie the further techniques of the other kinds of comparative linguistics, and one form or another of such "descriptive metacomparisons" must be applied in developing metacomparative techniques for .212, .22 and .31–4.

The applications themselves may differ in the orientation of the final statement required: in historical linguistics, for example, .221 (or .223), what demands summarily quantifying is the *difference* between etats (or histories), in typology the object will be *summation* of differentia. To such differences of emphasis will correspond degrees of recursion of metacomparison.

At this point an alternative branching of the interconnections of procedures presents itself. Reference has been made in 1.212 to criteria for typology represented by textual correspondences (n. 6, p. 20); if the relative frequency of such correspondences were made the basis of a "typological index" (in a quite different sense from Greenberg's), one would be proceeding not from or through 2.2222–3 but directly from 2.2221.

Similarly, "historical metacomparison", which was already inherent in 1.223 (n. 11, p. 21) as well as 1.224, may either proceed from 2.2222 or conceivably exploit the unidirectional relation of historical succession[75] by proceeding from 2.2223, distinguishing "ease of transition" in the two (–TA→ -type) directions (–S→ at all levels) between etats.

The quantification of genetic comparison is not exhausted by the possible common techniques of metacomparison, for the reasons given in 1.32, requiring also handling of probabilities and weighting of data for relevance to language-identity and -relation. But in drawing on directly systemic simple and comparative descriptive

[74] n. 39 above. Cf. M. A. K. Halliday, "The Tones of English", *Archivum Linguisticum*, XV, pp. 1–28 (p. 2).
[75] Cf. J. Holt, *Proceedings of the Seventh International Congress of Linguists, London, 1952*, p. 98.

linguistics for identification of its comparabilia, it may in any case utilize the metacomparative processes based in .211 (but cf. n. 71).

With the genetic relation of languages not at stake, "convergence metacomparison" presents an essentially simpler probability picture, in calling not for a quantification of "yes-no (how likely)" but for some formulation of "*degree* of convergence" of one set of contiguous languages as compared with another (cf. references in n. 38 on p. 29) or (in subclassifying within one set) of a pair A and B with the pairs A and C or B and C.[76] But the problem remains, as in general typology, of the weight to be attached to a given category or set of exponents at a given degree of delicacy, no evident way yet offering itself of equating automatically degrees of delicacy at different points (i.e. differentiated at primary delicacy) on the syntagmatic axis (let alone, in linear/textual comparison, between different languages, n. 39).

Thus if for example in subclassifying the Balkan languages more weight were put on the postposed definite article than on *have* + past participle expounding Perfect, Rumanian, Albanian and Macedonian would to that extent be classed with Bulgarian rather than with Greek, if the reverse with Greek rather than with Bulgarian; that the allocation would differ at different degrees of delicacy of comparison and classification is to be expected, but the definition of these degrees in terms of grammatical categories and delicacy remains problematical.

Again, different results might be obtained by equal-systemic and one-way systemic system-reductions, though as in single-language (or non-genetic language-comparative) historical linguistics the latter has evident relevance in reflecting the diachronic process (of spread of specific convergence features).

Nor does "convergence metacomparison" escape quantitative (probability) problems of genetic identification of phonological (or graphological) exponence (or of formal item expounded (calquing)), as regards individual items. In applying here, for example, the "numeral index" method of 2.2222–3, the difficulty mentioned in

---

[76]   Cf. Ellis, "Possible Comparisons", p. 299 (Appendix F, pp. 152-3).

n. 64 (discrepancy of phonological and graphological) is extended to discrepancy between synchronic (even graphological) number of items/correspondences (e.g. Rumanian *şaizeci* (older *şasezeci*), 60, beside *şase*, 6, a separate item/correspondence from *şaptezeci*, 70, etc. (beside *şapte*, 7, etc.)) and what is genetically identical (e.g. *şase*(-) and *şai*-); or again the merging into one item/correspondence of what is (e.g. Rumanian *-sprezece*, Bulgarian -найсет, Albanian *-mbë-dhjetë* (for 11–19 "-teen")) and is not (e.g. these and Turkish *ón* –) a possible exponential calque (here "upon ten") – these are of course immediately resolvable by giving procedural priority to the genetic or historical linguistics of language-families involved (e.g. Slavonic among Balkan languages) or individual languages, *if* this provides certain enough results for the given case: with such cases as the numerals it may be expected to, with some other cases not, and the formulator of the theoretical framework of "convergence metacomparison" must face the need for a cline on which "certain enough" is a cut-off in some degree arbitrary.

Finally, Balkan linguistics, for example, has now in principle attained a delicacy of comparison where varieties within the languages, registers, figure with growing prominence[77]; the utilization of this in "convergence metacomparison" involving weighting of of, or by, register-features will be one of the products of development of "dialectology etc.", and of its interactions with the other kinds of comparative linguistics, within the theoretical framework of specialized comparative linguistics, and of the articulation and integration of comparative linguistics generally.

[77] E.g. S. Heřman's paper to the Fifth International Congress of Slavists, Sofia, 1963: "Počátky spisovné bulharštiny a její poměr k sousedním jazykům na Balkáně do konce XIX století".

APPENDICES

GENERAL NOTE ON APPENDICES

Four of these seven Appendices, B, C, F, G, have been published previously, and the author is very grateful to the previous publishers for permission to reprint; another, E, was also written before this book was projected. These five have been slightly revised, and in particular to references to B, C, F, G themselves have been added explicit references to the pagination of this book: such additional matter is enclosed in square brackets.

The revisions in the second half of Appendix C owe much to the kind comments of Professor K. Jackson (who however has no responsibility for the new formulations). The author is also very grateful to Dr. R. Huddleston for his comments on Appendix A in draft. Appendix A has also benefited from discussion with Dr. M. A. K. Halliday, but the particular formulations are the author's own responsibility.

The previous places of publication of B, C, F, G are as follows:

B: *Lingua*, VII (1958), pp. 134–174.
C: *Proceedings of the University of Durham Philosophical Society*, Volume I, Series B (Arts), No. 7 (1961), pp. 54–62.
F: *Славянска Филология*, Bulgarian Committee of Slavists (for Fifth International Congress of Slavists) (Sofia, 1963), Volume III, pp. 291–9.
G: *Studia Linguistica in honorem Acad. S. Mladenov* (Sofia, Bulgarian Academy of Sciences, 1957), pp. 555–565.

Appendix A

THEORY OF DESCRIPTIVE LINGUISTICS

Since comparison of languages presupposes description of each language, a theory of comparative linguistics presupposes a theory of descriptive linguistics. Techniques of comparison as outlined here could, to a varying extent,[1] be operated using descriptions according to any theory; but the descriptive theory and terminology specifically followed here (above and Appendices D, E, F) is that expounded by M. A. K. Halliday in "Categories of the Theory of Grammar", *Word*, 17 (1961), pp. 241–292. Reference should be made to this and other works of Halliday (above, n. 4, p. 12; n. 74, p. 58, and "Class in Relation to the Axes of Chain and Choice in Language", *Linguistics*, 2, 1963, pp. 5–15, "Lexis as a Linguistic Level", in *In Memory of J. R. Firth*); R. M. W. Dixon, "A Logical Statement of Grammatical Theory", *Language*, 39, (1963), pp. 654–68; J. M. Sinclair, "Beginning the Study of Lexis", and J. Ellis, "On Contextual Meaning", both in *In Memory of J. R. Firth*; the following is merely a brief account of some of the terms employed above (especially 1.31, 2.1, 2.21) and of definitionally related ones.

Alterinterlevel: An interlevel linking a level (form) with an alternative level (substance).

Alternative level: One of the two (or conceivably more[2]) kinds of substance, phonic or graphic . . .

[1] To some extent other theories generate their own techniques of comparison, e.g. S. Lamb, "Stratificational Linguistics as a Basis for Mechanical Translation", U.S.–Japan Seminar on MT, Tokyo, April 1964.

[2] By this is not meant encodings of one or the other of the two usual alternative levels or interlevels, e.g. Braille (as conventionally devised) or the "hearing glove": the nearest to existing examples would be a second graphological interlevel for Chinese/Japanese (the relation to the alternative interlevels varying slightly with

Category: The theory of grammar has four categories, unit, class, system, structure. Unit is not variable on the scale of delicacy, but the other three include more and more delicate categories, so that a grammatical item (see Formal Item) is statable as exponent of a category.

Class: One of the four categories of the theory of grammar (and phonology). Classes are of a unit (and thus help to link units with delicacy), and are exponents of elements of structure (see Rank). Systems are of classes.

Context: The interlevel between form and situation, and a terminal level of language (cf. above, n. 5 on p. 34), relating grammatical and lexical items to extra-linguistic features (see Meaning).

Delicacy: One of the scales. See above, 2.1, 2.221 (n. 47), n. 39 on p. 44. As a scale in the theory of grammar it links class, system and structure with more and less delicate classes, systems and structures respectively and hence the general categories of the theory with the data of a given language.

Demilevel: A division of the level of form, see Grammar, Lexis.

Element of structure: The structure of a unit has elements which occur in places, e.g. (see above, n. 33, p. 42) S,P,C,A are elements of primary structure of the English clause, which occur respectively at places 2; 4; 5 and 6; 1, 3 and 7 of the clause-structure ASAPCCA (e.g. "Naturally he never gave them things quickly.").

Exponence: One of the scales. Items of substance are said to be exponents of phonological or graphological items or categories, phonological (graphological) items or categories exponents of phonological (graphological) categories, phonological (graphological) items or categories exponents of formal items or categories, formal items or categories exponents of formal categories.

Form: A primary level, and the central level. Within it items or categories which have contextual meaning (see Meaning) are

---

the particular alphabetization), with its alternative graphic substance, and independent components of deaf and dumb "language" (insofar as they do relate to the level of form of say English but not to its orthography). (There is clearly a cline (partly of institutionalization), with e.g. shorthand intermediate, between being and not being a separate alternative level.)

treated according to their relation to each other (formal meaning). It is divided into the two demilevels, grammar and lexis. The criterion for this division may be formulated in a number of (formal) ways,[3] but the central one appears to be that grammar is concerned with closed systems, and lexis with what this leaves over of form, namely items in open sets ("fully lexical items") and members of closed systems ("grammatical items") inasmuch as they may be associated with open-set items. On the transition between grammar and lexis see Grammar.

Formal item: Practically characterizable as the "things" that the linguistic analyst (at the level of form) handles (e.g. "the word *man*", "apostrophe *s*"), the formal item is perhaps best definable theoretically as a nexus between relations of exponence, that which expounds the categories of form (member of a lexical set, or the more complex categories of grammar) and is expounded by a phonological or graphological item.

Grammar: One of the two demilevels of form. See Form, Categories, Scales. The relative theoretical power of grammar is such that the linguistic analyst will seek to extend the application of grammatical analysis to the maximum ("grammarian's dream"), leaving the minimum to the essentially statistical methods of lexis. Thus the scale of delicacy in grammar is terminated only when a grammatical class cannot be further subdivided into classes with

---

[3] The criterion expounded by W. A. C. H. Dobson, *Late Archaic Chinese* (Toronto, 1959), *Early AC* (Toronto, 1962), to distinguish the cenematic and plerematic words of Classical Chinese, namely that the former have fixed or limited distribution (in the "sentence"), cannot be generalized to languages of other grammatical types without reformulation in more involved terms (concerning distribution of exponents of lexical items as exponents of stem-morphemes of grammatical classes of words), and moreover may result in a different dividing-line from other criteria (e.g. numerals plerematic), as well as possibly implying reverse priorities ("plerematic and grammatic*ized* usage") from the "grammarian's dream" (see Grammar) (and indeed is demonstrated, *Early*, by lexis-reminiscent statistics of grammatical distribution of plerematic words), but it does point to specifically linguistic aspects of the bifurcation of form not explicit in the logical distinction between closed/systemic and open: aspects more fully formulated by grammar's distinctive possession of the categories of structure and class, and of a kind of scale of rank, and categories of unit and system, distinct from anything lexical analysis may be shown to require.

demonstrably different structural, or systemic, behaviour: if this is before the class has become a one-member class (exponent a "grammatical item"),the exponents of the class will be "lexical items".

Graphic: see Substance.

Graphology: One of the two alterinterlevels, relating graphic substance and form.

Interlevel: A level linking primary levels and analysable only in dependence on them, though having its own categories.

Level: The linguistic analysis has three primary levels, substance (phonic or graphic), form, and situation, and interlevels between form and substance – phonology/graphology – and between form and situation – context. (Cf. above, n. 3 on p. 33.)

Lexis: One of the demilevels of form. Lexis is concerned with the collocation of formal items, i.e. with their occurrence in proximity (at different degrees) to each other irrespective of the structural relations of grammar. Meaningful statements of collocation demand large samples of text and statistical methods. This kind of analysis may be made to embrace not only "fully lexical items" (see Grammar), but any formal items; and the findings of lexical analysis also need to be correlated with the grammatical analysis of the same text (lexicogrammatical analysis). The exponent of a lexical item may coincide with the exponent of any morpheme or other unit of grammar or combination thereof (cf. also above, 2.1, p. 33, on phonaesthetics); whether or not lexical items may be shown to compose larger lexical items, they lack, by definition, any relation as complex as the rank-scale and associated categories of grammar.

Meaning: The relation of linguistic items or categories, to each other (formal meaning, the relation of formal items or categories to each other, paradigmatically in systems or syntagmatically in structures, and similarly phonological meaning, the relation of phonological items or categories to each other) or to components of situation (contextual meaning of formal items or categories).

Phonic: see Substance.

Phonology: One of the two alterinterlevels, relating phonic substance and form.

Place in structure: see Element.

Primary (grammatical) *delicacy*: the first stage of grammatical delicacy, at which just sufficient distinctions of class, system and structure are made to provide a chain-exhausting (syntagmatically exhaustive) account of the given unit.

Primary level: A level analysable independently of other levels.

Rank: One of the scales. It links units (grammatical or phonological) with each other through classes of units as exponents of elements of structure.

Scale: The theory of grammar has three[4] scales of abstraction relating the categories to each other and to the data (cf. above, 2.1), rank, exponence and delicacy. There are also scales of rank and exponence in phonology and scales of delicacy at all levels (and cf. above, 2.221). Exponence also extends between levels.

Secondary delicacy: Any stage of delicacy after primary.

Situation: A (terminal) level of linguistic analysis, but not of language. Components of situation, from which contextual meanings for a given language select (dependent upon the formal end), may be stated generally for all languages.

Structure: One of the four categories of the theory of grammar (and phonology). Any unit but the lowest has structure, and any unit but the highest is exponent of an element of structure of the unit next above, or, in grammar, of a unit lower than that – this is termed rank-shift. See Element. In recursive structures one element is in the same relation to another as that to a third, or in recursive rank-shift as one element of its structure to another. Recursive structures have a scale of depth.

Substance: One of the primary (and terminal) levels. See Alternative Levels. Like situation, substance may be described generally for all languages, e.g. phonic substance by general phonetics, but unlike situation, firstly substance is a small part of the observable world, and secondly the selection from it made by a given language, described e.g. in the descriptive phonetics of a language, is partial, some features of substance not appearing at all in any one language

---

[4] Depth, sometimes given as a fourth scale, is dependent on rank in a way that none of the three scales is dependent on another. See Structure.

(as all situational components at any degree of delicacy can in the contextual meanings, at some degree of delicacy of reference, of any language), and not a mere selection of distinctions as in contextual meaning, and the selection of distinctions made by the phonology of a given language is partly dependent on this initial substantial selection.

System: One of the four categories of the theory of grammar (and phonology). In the general sense a closed set the (formal) meaning of any member of which would be changed by the addition or subtraction of a member, in the strict sense a system is such a set of classes (at some degree of delicacy) which are exponents of the same element of structure (at some degree of delicacy).

Unit: One of the four categories of the theory of grammar (and phonology). Theoretically a unit is defined by the existence of at least one unit above or below it on a scale of rank such that classes of a unit are exponents of elements of structure of another unit (see Structure). In practice, all languages so far closely examined have been found to require in grammar five[5] units, termable in description sentence (highest), clause, group, word, morpheme (lowest).

---

[5] As a minimum: it may be possible to establish structures above the sentence justifying the establishment of at least one higher unit.

Appendix B

GENERAL LINGUISTICS AND COMPARATIVE PHILOLOGY*

Introduction

W. S. Allen's "Relationship in Comparative Linguistics" (*Transactions of the Philological Society*, 1953, pp. 52–108) undoubtedly raises points of decisive importance for the present development of linguistics. One of them is the relation between comparative philology and general linguistics, for it is in the name of the latter that Allen makes the criticisms he does of the former. His position represents an extreme development of a cleavage which has had some existence for the last half-century (I). It is not the object of the present article to review at length the history of views on the subject, but rather to examine the validity of Allen's view.[1]

Comparative philology may be defined as the comparison of languages (through comparison of items within them) that are, or are assumed to be, genetically related, with the object of establishing such relationships and of reconstructing original forms from which derivation may be made (II).

It therefore assumes that it is possible to establish, or at least to attribute a meaning to, genetic relation of languages or of linguistic

* Thanks are due, for assistance throughout to Dr. P. Wexler and Dr. M. A. K. Halliday, for discussion of the material also to T. Hill, W. B. Lockwood and H. D. Berg, and for comments, criticisms and suggestions, to Professor W. S. Allen, J. Atkinson, Dr. C. Baier, Professor C. E. Bazell, A. Binns, Professor I. M. Campbell, Professor M. Cohen, N. Collinge, R. A. Crossland, Mrs M. 'Espinasse, Professor J. R. Firth, W. Haas, Professor A. S. C. Ross, M. L. Samuels, Professor A. Scherer, Professor S. Ullmann, Dr. A. Wolf, Dr. P. Worsley, and particularly Dr. A. Vos.
[1] Allen's "Phonetics and Comparative Linguistics", *Archivum Linguisticum*, 3 (1951), pp. 126–136, is less far-reaching but contains already some indication of his more elaborated views.

items, and derivation of one from another (III); and that the construction of hypothetical forms is valid in some sense (IV).

Allen denies that these are possible within scientific linguistics (as at present known), and therefore ("whilst recognizing its own unassailable status and value") opposes the inclusion of comparative philology within scientific linguistics (at present) (V).

This characterization of comparative philology constitutes a step beyond the antinomizing of historical linguistics and synchronic linguistics inaugurated by Saussure. It is a step into intolerance ("within scientific linguistics") of historical linguistics by non-historical linguistics.

That the Saussurean position on this question is unsatisfactory (though of course an advance on the exclusively historical conception of linguistics) is not in dispute; but, as the following argument will attempt to show, Allen's step appears to be in the wrong direction.

Comparative philology is a kind of historical linguistics, and one of the reasons why Allen denies the scientific character of comparative philology is that he denies the scientific character of historical linguistics. But comparative philology is also a kind of comparative linguistics, and Allen does not deny the scientific character of comparative linguistics in general.[2]

It is most important that we should separate from judgment of Allen's appraisal of comparative philology in the usual sense (as defined above)[3] and of historical linguistics, judgment of his proposals for comparative linguistics in a more general sense, i.e. comparison of languages irrespective of genetic relationship, with one or other object that may be classified as "descriptive" (VI). We also propose to consider (what Allen naturally ignores) how far the methods of comparative descriptive linguistics might be extended within a comprehensive comparative linguistics to comparative

---

[2] Allen might be said to confuse two kinds of comparative linguistics by associating "relation" (not, say, "correspondence") with the kind other than comparative philology (and with "Comparative Linguistics" in general in his title). Cf. VI and VII.

[3] And see II, n. 25.

philology (genetic comparative linguistics), and conversely the utility of comparative philology in more general linguistics (VII).

I. *The Nature of General Linguistics and the Supposed Antinomy of Historical and Synchronic Linguistics*

"He [Kruisinga] was not a philologist, neither in the continental, nor in the English sense of the word. He was a linguist, and used to insist on the distinction with his usual acerbity. 'There are philologists' he used to say '... who do not know there exists such a thing as linguistics'." P. A. Erades, "In Memoriam", *Lingua*, I, p. 142.

"General linguistics" is a term currently used with more than one meaning, however unaware some of those using it may be of the ambiguity; and it might be suggested that Allen is making use of this ambiguity in constructing in effect a syllogism in which the expression "general linguistics" masks an undistributed middle term:–
  a) All linguistics follows the principles of "general linguistics$_1$".
  b) "General linguistics$_2$" is "scientific" in a certain sense.
  Therefore c) All linguistics should be "scientific" in this same sense.

And comparative philology is not "scientific" in this sense (does not follow the same principles as "general linguistics$_2$"), therefore comparative philology is not part of linguistics.

What exactly is understood by "scientific" we shall examine in V. Here we are concerned to distinguish the senses of "general linguistics".

They may be defined as follows:

(1) The body of theory guiding work in all branches of linguistics.

(2) The branch of linguistics treating what is general to all languages (at all times).[4] Or, the body of theory guiding some branches of work in all languages.

As regards (1) there is of course the apparent "dilemma" stated by R. H. Robins.[5] "Linguistics is, in this respect, on the horns of a dilemma. Theory and theoretical discourse are empty unless they

[4] Cf. Allen, p. 87, "... general in a sense in which General Linguistics is general ... not restricted to the IE field ..." (cf. VII).
[5] "Noun and Verb in Universal Grammar", *Language*, 28, pp. 289–98 (pp. 297–98).

find application in the study of actual languages; on the other hand it must be admitted, even by those who most strongly assert that linguistics is a technique for the analysis of languages, that continuous examination is necessary, both of current doctrines explicitly formulated, and especially of the implicit and unstated tenets, for example of universal features, that influence our analytical operations".

It is true that one may base one's theory of a particular subject not only on the facts with which it deals but also on a more general theory covering other subjects too, as suggested by Allen ("linguistics in the past has generally kept in step with contemporary movements in other sciences", with references, p. 54, n. 2). But of course his "contemporary movements" are not the only possible general theory, as will be seen in V.

However, what we can say with certainty is that there is no necessity for *all* the principles of one branch of linguistics (e.g. of "general linguistics$_2$") to be common to all branches (constituting "general linguistics$_1$").

"General linguistics$_2$" is otherwise known as "Descriptive Linguistics".[6] That the term General Linguistics gets restricted to this branch of Linguistics is understandably due to the fact that explicit relation to General Linguistics$_1$ has so far been confined to Descriptive Linguistics, with some exceptions including Allen's explicitly negative relation of comparative philology.

Descriptive Linguistics is systemic. Its "principal aim", says W. Haas,[7] reviewing the present state of descriptive linguistic studies, is "to describe the utterances of a language in terms of intralingual relations. [Note that neither "utterances" nor "intralingual" in the sense they are here used could be applied to comparative philology (cf. on "utterances" II, III and VI, on "intralingual" III).] Descriptive Linguistics has come to be Structural Linguistics: all elements of speech (phonological, lexical, and grammatical) are now to be

[6] The term "linguistic analysis", at present applied to what descriptive linguistics does, would cover better the first of the alternative definitions given above of General Linguistics$_2$, if this is to include the diachronic generalities envisaged below.

[7] "On defining linguistic units", *TPS*, 1954, pp. 54–84 (p. 54).

defined and classified in terms of their relations to one another".[8]

That this systemic nature is a property of language and not merely of linguistic science is shown by Firth when he says[9] "Language and personality are built into the body which is constantly taking part in activities directed to the conservation of the pattern of life. We must expect . . . that linguistic science will also find it necessary to postulate the maintenance of linguistic patterns and systems (including adaptation and change) within which there is order, structure and function. Such systems are maintained by activity, and in activity they are to be studied. It is on these grounds that linguistics must be systemic".

According to Saussure, systemicness characterizes only language in its state at a given time, and not its history; or, to put it the other way round, only the atomic units[10] of a language have a history, not the system.[11] There are thus, according to Saussure, two separate linguistic sciences, the synchronic or systemic (or structural),[12] and the historical or atomistic.[13]

---

[8] Cf. – besides F. de Saussure, *Cours de linguistique générale*, 3rd edition (Paris, 1949), p. 116: "la langue est un système de pures valeurs que rien ne détermine en dehors de l'état momentané de ses termes", etc. – J. R. Firth, "General Linguistics and Descriptive Grammar", *TPS*, 1951, pp. 69–87 (esp. pp. 73–4); A. Reichling, "What is General Linguistics?", *Lingua*, I, pp. 8–24 (p. 13): "Each language is a system, all the parts of which co-operate and hang together organically . . ." and his observation that this was expressed by Gabelentz in 1891 [before Meillet's famous dictum "un langage forme un système très délicate et très compliqué où tout se tient rigoureusement . . .", *Année sociologique*, 8 (1903–4), p. 641].

[9] "The Semantics of Linguistic Science", *Lingua*, I, pp. 393–4 (p. 398).

[10] On "units" or "items" cf. n. 42 in III.

[11] *Cours* passim, e.g. pp. 114–129 (p. 116: "La multiplicité des signes, déjà invoquée pour expliquer la continuité de la langue, nous interdit absolument d'étudier simultanément les rapports dans le temps et les rapports dans le système"), p. 140, p. 185 ("qui dit grammatical dit synchronique").

[12] The terms "structure" and "system" will here be used in the Firthian sense (structure linear; system commutational, generally multidimensional) defined by R. H. Robins, "Formal Divisions in Sundanese", *TPS*, 1953, pp. 109–142 (p. 109, n. 2) (cf. J. R. Firth, *Proceedings of the VIIth International Congress of Linguists* (1952), London, 1956, p. 231); but "structural" is conventionally used with "linguistics" (etc.).

[13] "When MM. Bally and Sechehaye in 1916 apprised us of De Saussure's distinction between diachronic and synchronic linguistics, they taught Kruisinga

Not all linguists have been satisfied with this cleavage, or "antinomie criante", as R. Jakobson has called it,[14] and he and N. Trubetzkoy endeavoured to resolve it by introducing teleology into the development of systems instead of causation by accidental atomic changes.[15] This was an attempt to synthesize structural and historical linguistics without sacrificing the essence of one or the other.

---

nothing he did not know before. They only formulated a difference which Kruisinga had observed." (*Lingua*, I, p. 14).

[14] "Remarques sur l'évolution phonologique du russe", *TCLP*, 2 (1929), p. 13, in a passage worth quoting at length: "Schleicher conciliait la reconnaissance du sens interne fonctionnel du système linguistique, fournie par l'expérience directe, avec l'idée du manque de sens et du hasard aveugle de l'évolution de la langue, en interpretant ledit sens interne et fonctionnel comme un reste d'une perfection originaire du système linguistique. De ce point de vue l'évolution se réduit à une désagrégation, à une destruction. Une fois que le mythe romantique d'une époque indo-européenne commune comme d'un âge d'or de la langue eut été rayé de la science, l'antinomie apparut à découvert. Les néo-grammariens allemands ont reporté cette contradiction hors des limites de la linguistique, en déclarant que la science de la langue se borne à l'histoire de celle-ci ... Chez Saussure, qui a réhabilité la linguistique synchronique, l'antinomie devient criante et est érigé en dogme." Cf. S. Ullmann, *The Principles of Semantics* (London, 1951), pp. 142–4, 168.

[15] Saussure, *op. cit.*, p. 126 f.: "Chaque coup d'échecs ne met en mouvement qu'une seule pièce; de même dans la langue les changements ne portent que sur des éléments isolés ... Le déplacement d'une pièce est un fait absolument distinct de l'équilibre précédent et de l'équilibre subséquent. Le changement opéré n'appartient à aucun de ces deux états: or les états sont seuls importants ... Pour que la partie d'échecs ressemblât en tout point au jeu de la langue, il faudrait supposer un joueur inconscient ou inintelligent."

Jakobson, *loc. cit.*: "Dans l'interprétation de la diachronie, Saussure se rattache étroitement aux traditions scientifiques du XIXe siècle ... Ainsi se creuse un fossé profond entre la linguistique diachronique et la linguistique synchronique, la brillante comparaison de Saussure entre le jeu de la langue et une partie d'échecs perd sa force persuasive si l'on se range à l'opinion de Saussure affirmant que la langue ne prémédite rien et que ses pièces se déplacent fortuitement." Cf. J. R. Firth, "Structural Linguistics", *TPS*, 1955, pp. 83–103 (p. 91).

Cf. the references at Allen, p. 104 (nn. 2 and 3), and Allen himself in his earlier work (our Introduction, n. 1), p. 129, "the value of structuralism in comparative and historical study is not to be denied", and p. 130 (nn. 3, 4 and 5). Also H. M. Hoenigswald, "The Principal Step in Comparative Grammar", *Language*, 23 (1950), pp. 357–64 (p. 364); Z. S. Harris, "Distributional Structure" (Martinet, *Linguistics Today* (*Publications of Linguistic Circle of New York – No. 2*), New York, 1954 (= *Word*, Vol. 10, No. 2–3), pp. 26–42), p. 27, n l.

Now it appears that W. S. Allen wishes to unify linguistic science by excluding historical study from science.[16] We shall endeavour to show (in V) that in any case comparative philology *is* a science. But there remains the question how far the science of linguistics, including comparative philology, is unified, how far the principles of General Linguistics$_1$ extend.

Synchronic linguistics is (among other things), as an account of linguistic system, an abstraction from successive acts of speech, constituting, in their entirety, concrete linguistic history.[17] In this sense it is an abstraction from the material of diachronic linguistics, "diachronic linguistic reality" (cf. Reichling, *Lingua*, I, p. 15). It is true that diachronic linguistics itself must be methodologically secondary to (built upon) the synchronic linguistics of various periods, i.e. a further abstraction from it, two removes from diachronic reality; but can the synchronic abstraction from diachronic reality be scientific without the further diachronic abstraction from it, if this latter has (as Allen says it has[18]) any validity at all, being scientific also? (Of course, we are here appealing to *objective* criteria of scientificness (relation to "reality"), as opposed to Allen's positivistic criteria, on which see V.)

And can the synchronic abstraction be systemic without the further diachronic abstraction from it having some relation to system? It is of course apparent that linguistic system is essentially synchronic, or rather "out of time", [19] in the sense that in the

---

[16] P. 102: "it may be that, whilst recognizing its own unassailable status and value, one should hesitate to admit historical linguistics to membership of the general linguistic disciplines, or to [sic] do so only in so far as it enters into a descriptive comparatism"; and p. 106: "I see no alternative, within the present framework of general linguistic and scientific method, to a comparatism in which time has no direction and there is no becoming".

[17] This is not to dispute Firth above (ref. in n. 9); on the contrary his conception is a ground for attributing "system" to *history*. Cf. the reference to his "Personality and Language in Society" in IV, n. 79.

[18] pp. 54, 91–2 (III, n. 50).

[19] See the reference to Firth at Allen, p. 106, n. 3. Cf. Firth, "Structural Linguistics", p. 91: "Meillet, who added to 'système', the emphatic clause 'où tout se tient' [cf. n. 8], even found it possible to say 'le progres de la civilisation détruit le duel'."

history of a language (cf. III) one system is replaced by another.[20]
But this is not to say that a system has no history, or history has no
system.[21] The future task of general linguistics[1][22] would appear to
be to bring the phenomena of linguistic change, in abstraction from
comparative-philological[23] concreteness (cf. end of VII), into the
domain of systemic explanation.[24] Meanwhile the task cannot be

[20]   Cf. Saussure, *Cours*, pp. 112–3: "Le temps altère toutes choses; il n'y pas de
raison pour que la langue échappe à cette loi universelle . . . La langue est pour
nous le langage moins la parole: . . . le temps permettra aux forces sociales
s'exerçant sur elle de développer leurs effets . . ."
    I.e., successive acts of speech (*parole*) in a given community ultimately differ
so greatly as to imply different linguistic systems (*langue*). (On how far the
speed and extent of this differentiation may be determined by differentiation
e.g. of generations within the "community", cf. A. Scherer, "Worauf beruht die
Verschiedenheit der indogermanischen Sprachen?", *ZIF*, LXI, pp. 201–15 (pp.
212–214), and R. A. Hall, "Pidgin English and Linguistic Change", *Lingua*, III,
pp. 143–4).
[21]   Cf. the references at Allen, pp. 103–4. Also H. Vogt, "Contact of Languages"
(Martinet, *op. cit.* pp. 245–53), p. 247.
[22]   Reichling, *Lingua*, I, initial summary: "The empirical science of General
Linguistics aims at tracing and defining the universal categories of speech-
phenomena, as well as the factors on which these categories depend. It further
studies the non-universal categories of speech-phenomena, in their relationship
to the universal ones, especially and closely examing those universal factors
that control their existence and changes . . . General Linguistics therefore,
while establishing and studying as its chief object all that is systematic in speech
and language, must of necessity extend the scope of its investigations to the
diachronic phenomena as well."
[23]   Comparative philology itself, being only a part of diachronic linguistics
(cf. V, VII), does not require the systemicness in its synchronic material that
diachronic linguistics as a whole does (cf. III, n. 74, V, n. 103), but the above argument as to scientificness applies to it as to any part of diachronic linguistics.
[24]   A possible avenue for approaching this task, particularly if combined with a
structural conception of phonetic units (a systemic [specifically prosodic?]
definition of complexity, cf. IV), is the hypothesis of G. K. Zipf, in *The Psycho-
Biology of Language* (London, 1936), that a language maintains a negative correlation between the linear frequency of phonetic units and their relative "complexity", which would yield a chain of causation through the "levels of linguistic
analysis" from "social contextualization" (determining (semantically) the frequency of morphemes which happen to contain given phonetic units) to features
of articulation (as opposed to the atomistic view of phonetic accidents being
first [intralinguistic] cause). (On levels, Firth, "General Linguistics", p. 76
("hierarchy of linguistic techniques"); Haas, *TPS*, 1954, p. 83 ("hierarchy of
linguistic levels", and p. 82, n. 3 on Firth's "spectrum, model" seeming not to
provide for "the evident hierarchical order").) Cf. (besides C. C. Berg, *VIIth*

evaded of consolidating the position within general linguistics of the achievements to date of comparative philology.

II. *The Nature of Comparative Philology*

"It is the essence of the comparative discipline" says Allen (p. 57) "that it seeks to replace the intuitive recognition of similarities by a systematic analysis of their nature". He goes on to say that the elaboration of such a discipline began with such scholars as Bopp and Rask, and immediately moves on to "the techniques that we find ourselves employing today".

These he defines as comparison of items identified as comparable, which are "mainly" words or "more often" morphemes, "identified on a combined formal and semantic basis"; he then discusses the semantic and the formal bases in turn, arguing of each that it is inconclusive.

Here less than justice is done to the history of achievement in the science of comparative philology[25] since its foundation, to the objective reasons why the material of comparative philology consists in the units that it does, and to the essential process that comparative philology conducts with this material.

The evolution of comparative philology as a science (cf. V) has consisted in the development of a recognition in practice of what in language is relevant to the establishment of genetic relationship, and of making precise the techniques of utilizing it for this purpose. Admittedly the results of these techniques can never achieve the whole truth: it is true, as Allen says (p. 64f., cf. p. 76), that the dis-

---

Congress, p. 401) J. Fourquet, "Die Nachwirkungen der ersten und der zweiten Lautverschiebungen", *Zeitschrift für Mundartforschung*, XXII (1954), pp. 1–33 (p. 33): "die Kräfte, die vom *signatum* her die Struktur beeinflussen – z.B. die grössere 'Belastung' der verschiedenen Unterscheidungsmerkmale, lexikalische oder morphologische". In general on adding "why" to "how", A. Martinet, *VIIth Congress*, p. 459.

[25] The term "comparative philology" will be used here in accordance with traditional English usage (cf. Firth, *Lingua*, I, p. 396, n. 3, on the divergences from continental usage), rejecting Allen's distinction between linguistics and philology ("Phonetics", p. 136, with n. 2), which identifies "Comparative Philology, as a branch of Classical or other Philology" with the philology (*philologie*) that shows "how the letters of texts have changed" (cf. p. 132).

covery of Hittite necessitated drastic changes in the previous results for Indo-European; but there is progressive elimination of error: changes in Indo-European constructs were possible, and were made, that were consistent with (and explained) the relevant forms of Hittite – and the hypothesis of Indo-European relation was not disproved; on the contrary, it was further confirmed.

The aspect of language which reflects community of origin of two or more languages, as comparative philology has through observation of objective facts come to assume in its practice (and rightly, for reasons to be treated in III and IV), is the *phonetic* development,[26] or, more synchronically speaking, the results of the phonetic development, of the linguistic items[27] which have survived from the original (see III) in more than one of the languages,[28] material consisting of morphemes[29] or combinations of morphemes[30] "mainly" with "the upper limit for the item" of the "word"[31]

[26] The opening of Allen's "Phonetics" is therefore to be most heartily applauded: "'Comparative Grammar', the early title of the comparative discipline – and one which is still by no means moribund – does not suggest any specially close link between it and Phonetics. The purpose of this paper is to suggest why such a title is inherently inappropriate and to emphasize that a closer alliance with the phonetic discipline must form the basis of future advances in the comparative field".

[27] One therefore cannot accept Allen's ("Phonetics", second paragraph and p. 128, second paragraph) denial to morphology of a place in the comparative method. Cf. A. W. de Groot, "Structural Linguistics and Phonetic Law", *Lingua*, I, pp. 175–208 (p. 208): "The regularity of the phonetic laws lies in quite a different stratum from that of the phonemes. It is a regularity not of phonemic systems, but of word-form systems".

[28] Cf. (as opposed to Allen, p. 87) J. Gonda, "The Comparative Method as applied to Indonesian Languages", *Lingua*, I, pp. 86–101 (p. 88): "the existence, in a number of languages, of groups of words, categories of forms, etc., which show regular points of resemblance etc., cannot be due to mere accident; it must be explained from special causes, the most important of which is genetical relationship ... We conclude that this relationship exists from regular points of resemblance and constant differences, which can neither be explained by borrowing nor by certain properties or developments which are peculiar to human spirit in general".

[29] A. I. Smirnitsky, *Sravnitel'no-istorichesky metod i opredelenie yazykovogo rodstva* (Moscow, 1955), pp. 25–6.

[30] Smirnitsky, p. 27.

[31] An example above this limit is furnished by the initial mutations of Celtic, which originated in certain syntagmas. [See Appendix C.]

(Allen, p. 57).[32] Of course the concepts involved here remain in need of further refinement (for the formulation of the phonetic development see IV, for the [lexical and grammatical] scope of the "items" see III), but there is no retreating from the fact established by over a century of comparative philological practice that phonetic habits show regularities of development.

What comparative philology has learned to do with this material is something more solid than might be the impression from Allen's separation "for analytical purposes" of the "two aspects of the identification".[33] According to Allen (p. 60) "by one means or another, the semantic identification is made. But without the restriction of simultaneous formal identification the number of possible comparisons would, of course, be unlimited; only those semantic equations are therefore considered for which it proves possible to state a corresponding formal equation . . ." It would be less misleading to say that the comparative philologist (actually a succession of generations of comparative philologists) observes within one language a number of morphemes or combinations of morphemes each of which from its meaning (lexical or grammatical) has some possibility of being of the same origin (that is, of having had the same meaning originally) as one in another language, and each of which from its phonetic structure has some possibility of being of the same origin (that is, of having had the same phonetic structure originally) as the same one in the other language, and that the latter possibility, and therefore the former possibility, *is raised*[34]

---

[32] "Des analogies de structure, même grandes, si elles ne sont pas accompagnées de faits particuliers significatifs, ne prouvent pas une parenté de langues". (A. Meillet, *Linguistique historique et linguistique générale*, I, second edition, Paris, 1926, p. 26; cf. *Introduction*[1], c.p. 24; and Hall, *Lingua*, III, p. 145 on "brusque non-evolutive re-structurings".) This is the answer to the position of Trubetzkoy quoted by Allen, p. 92, n. 2.

[33] But cf. "Phonetics", p. 129: "it was the great merit of the Neogrammarians that, unlike Schleicher, they attributed the contradictions not to linguistic irregularity but to false identification. Henceforth the formal correspondences possessed that quality of regularity and predictability which marked them off from the functional correspondences".

[34] A mathematical formulation of the astronomical degrees of probability involved is offered by E. Polivanov (*Za Marksistskoe Yazykoznanie*, 1931) in his refutation of N. Y. Marr's implied claim that the correspondences of comparative

to an overwhelming probability[35] when the phonetic developments requiring to be assumed for each are the same for all. (And it is in this *relation between* the two, not brought out by Allen, that the essence of the method lies (cf. Smirnitsky, p. 25).) In other words, there is no absolute "identification" of any one individual item, as Allen implies is claimed, but there is scientific certainty (cf. V) that an accumulation of items are of identical origin.[36] Allen admits the coherence of the technique when he says, p. 60, "congruent with those set up for other acceptable equations", and p. 61, "identical phoneme by phoneme in accordance with the established system of correspondences, to which they themselves add support", but how the "established system", the "acceptable equations", have come to be established he does not discuss; "only corroborative items are accepted", he says, as if the "correspondence-systems" e.g. of Indo-European had been woven out of fancy. Of course there will always be borderline cases (Allen pp. 62–3), but their dubiety does not affect the certainty of the decisive mass, and the border of certain knowledge is always shifting.

"The essence of the comparative discipline" then is not merely, as Allen says, the "*systematic analysis* of the nature of similarities" (our italics) but the establishment of the particular objective significance of *certain* (originally "intuitively recognized") "similarities".[37]

---

philology are coincidence. Cf. P. Thieme, "Die Heimat der indogermanischen Grundsprache", *Ak. der Wiss. u. der Lit.*, *Geistes- u. Sozialwiss. Cl.*, Mainz, *Jg.* 1953, *Nr.* 11, pp. 535–613), II (Anhang), B., "Die Hypothese einer einheitlichen Grundsprache", p. 595: the alternative "vestige of" possibility is "so federleicht zu wiegen, als ob er gar nicht vorhanden wäre".

[35] See my "Further Note on the Soviet Linguistics Controversy" *Soviet Studies*, III (1951), p. 174, and A. S. C. Ross, "Philological Probability Problems" *Journal of the Royal Statistical Society*, Series B, vol. XII (1950), pp. 19–59 (p. 21).

[36] Cf. Smirnitsky, p. 29.

[37] In fact it is not a question of straightforward similarity, cf. Ross, *ibid.*, pp. 20, 58; Meillet, *LHLG*, I, p. 92, *Introduction* pp. 470–1: "l'histoire phonétique ne se fait pas avec des ressemblances, mais avec des systèmes de correspondances ... le linguiste n'opère pas avec des faits concrets plus ou moins homologues, mais avec des correspondances pouvant porter sur des faits hétérogènes."; Smirnitsky, p. 30.

It remains to add (the element of truth in Allen's exaggerated criticisms of comparative philology) that it is necessary not to forget the limits of application

III. *The Nature of Linguistic Identity and Genetic Relation*

But what is this objective significance, and why does it repose only in a certain aspect of language?

Two stages may be distinguished in the answer to this question: the genetic relation of individual *linguistic items* (a different matter from *establishability* with an individual item![38]); and the relatability of *whole languages*.[39]

The kind of linguistic items of which it is possible to assert genetic relation between individual items (i.e. irrespective of whether there is genetic relation of languages)[40] is more comprehensive than that (already provisionally defined in II) which provides evidence of genetic relation of languages. In fact, with the possible exception of grammatical morphemes as such,[41] any kind of item[42] from an

---

of this method (cf. Gonda, *Lingua*, I, pp. 88–9: "The method itself shows us the limits of its competency, it shows us that there are many questions that it cannot solve. It reveals to us a simplified development of the languages, it draws only in the rough. 'Il ne faut pas s'imaginer que, avec les correspondances simples, on touche la réalité des choses.' [Meillet] Reality has been a good deal more complicated than is revealed by our method which does not show the linguistic changes themselves. It may and must be complemented by studying along other lines."), and that as practised hitherto it is in need of critical revision at many points, cf. (besides Scherer, *ZIF*, LXI, especially p. 212) B. A. Serebrennikov, "O nedostatkakh sravnitel'no-istoricheskogo metoda v yazykoznanii", *Izvestiya Akademii Nauk: Otdelenie Literatury i Yazyka*, 1950, pp. 177 ff.); also J. Engels, *VIIth Congress*, pp. 411–23 (especially pp. 412, 423).

[38] See II. On the distinction between objective relatedness and its establishability cf. Allen pp. 74–5 and Gonda, *Lingua*, I, p. 88, and also the discussion of the ancillary function of comparative philology in V.

[39] We may agree with Allen p. 91 that one should start with the question, where does language *a* belong ? with the possibility of a multiple answer (i.e. where are we to relate items in the language), but it is no contradiction to go on to the question "Does language *a* (as a whole) belong to the family *A* or not?"

[40] Such individual items are shown in fact to be related not by the methods of comparative philology in the strict sense (see II) but by textual and extra-linguistic evidence.

[41] See below (n. 55) and cf. Meillet, *Introduction*, p. 36; Smirnitsky, p. 48; D. M. Jones, *TPS*, 1950, p. 68 ("very infrequent"); A. Sommerfelt, *VIIth Congress*, p. 458. But cf. U. Weinreich, *Languages in Contact, Findings and Problems* (= *Publications of the Linguistic Circle of New York*, No. 1) (New York, 1953), pp. 32–3 (Meglenite Rumanian personal endings from Bulgarian (p. 32), Georgian instrumental -*iw* from Armenian (p. 33, n. 13)), though some of his cases (Welsh

allophone[43] to a sentence,[44] and from a phonemic opposition[45] to a sentence-form,[46] may be genetically related to one in a language that may not be genetically related, i.e. one of them is "borrowed"[47] from the other language (at some earlier stage) or both from some other common source.

It is not clear whether Allen would admit this proposition within scientific linguistics. "We have a system A set up for L_x and a system B for L_y; but without transferring to the systems the in any case doubtful postulate of '$L_x > L_y$', how does one support the statement '$A > B$'?" (p. 103). But it is not a question of *transferring* from one to the other; each "postulate" has validity in its own right, as we shall see (and if anything we are suggesting that the "language"-one is based upon (*inter alia*) the "item"-one). Cf. de Groot, *Lingua*, I, p. 182: "that before and after the change we have to do with the same word. For the linguist this is not a question of identity in the objective sense, but of *continuity*. We are dealing with the same notion as when we wish to define interlinguistic relationship, i.e. when we wish to state that we are dealing with

---

plural -*s* from English (pp. 32–3), Rumanian vocative -*o* from Slavonic (p. 33, n. 13)) could be explained as spread of morphemes from whole word-forms borrowed.

[42] Comprising both Haas's *units* and *relations* between units (*TPS*, 1954, p. 56); cf. Firth, *Lingua*, I, p. 400 (point *e*): "A *speech event* may be sub-divided into *speech items*."

[43] e.g. non-pre-vocalic *r* consonantal pronounced (by some) in English in borrowings from French (bête noi*r*e) (in aphonematic terms (cf. IV, n. 96), an increase in the number of possibilities in position V–(C)).

[44] e.g. "Cherchez la femme". Cf. Weinreich, p. 46 ("Goraelli!").

[45] e.g. intermediate (non-palatalized clear [non-velar]) *l* pronounced in borrowings from French etc. (блёф) in one style of pre- (and immediately post-) Revolutionary Russian pronunciation.

[46] e.g. Irish English "Is it departed he is?".

[47] Cf. Weinreich and his bibliography; he objects to the term "borrowing" for interference with systems, "the rearrangement of patterns that result [*sic*] from the introduction of foreign elements into the more highly structured domains of language, such as the bulk of the phonemic system, a large part of the morphology and syntax, and some areas of the vocabulary (kinship, colour, weather, etc.). It would be an oversimplification to speak here of borrowing, or mere additions to an inventory." See his table of conditions, etc., pp. 64-5, and cf. H. Vogt, *op. cit.* (I, n. 21).

two periods of the same language . . . I should like to define this identity as identity for the consciousness of speakers and listeners". Cf. Allen, pp. 87–8.

It must be noted that whole groups of items[48] (with the exception as mentioned of grammatical morphemes) may be borrowed at one time.[49] In this case (as opposed to that in note 41), and if the items are such as to have a "phonetic structure" (II, IV), i.e. are morphemes or combinations of morphemes, their relation, or in other words the borrowing, may be established by the methods of comparative philology.[50]

What cannot (except between dialects[51]) be borrowed[52] as a whole are the features that constitute the specific identity of a language,[53] the "grammar"[54] and what we may call the "lexical basis".[55] "What constitutes the identity of a language (as distinct

[48] Possibly constituting the same system as in the source-language, so that items genetically relatable may include even large-scale systems. On how far syntax can be borrowed see VII (n. 139).

[49] Firth, "Sounds and Prosodies", *TPS*, 1948 (and references there); E. Henderson, "The Phonology of Loanwords in some South-East Asian Languages", *TPS*, 1951; my "Structure of Neologisms in Russian and Czech" (unpublished Ph. D. thesis, London, 1948) and (on Balkan syntax) *VIIth Congress*, p. 125.

[50] It will be seen that there need be no opposition between traditional comparative philology, the classification of languages by their origin (see below), and the classification of languages by the origin of some of their elements ("affinité phonologique", etc., "typology" in the Trubetzkoyan sense (cf. VII, n. 138)); they answer different questions.

But where in this does Allen's "practical identification of languages by groups" come? See V.

[51] e.g. Weinreich, p. 32, n. 9; cf. Thieme, p. 608.

[52] Into a *language*, as distinct from the speech of an *individual* (cf. Weinreich, p. 69, on "collapse" (of a unitary system) in individuals; p. 33, on speech as distinct from language).

[53] Cf. Scherer, *ZIF*, LXI, pp. 201–2 and n. 1: marked phonetic differences not enough. Cf. IV, n. 76.

[54] Cf. Meillet, *Introduction*, p. 32; so Weinreich, p. 15: morphemes most integrated in structure are least subject to transfer; cf. my "Structure of Neologisms" (n. 50), Chaps. VI & VII.

[55] Cf. A. Chikobava, *Vvedenie v Yazykoznanie*, Part I (Moscow, 1952), pp. 32–5, 91. A review of Chikobava by G. P. Springer and M. Zarechnak (*Language*, XXX, pp. 578–83) claims (p. 581, n. 5) that "Meillet had made similar observations at least thirty years earlier", and it is true that (*LHLG*, I, p. 24) he gives examples of grammatical morphemes showing relation, and (p. 82) he says "les systèmes grammaticaux de deux langues sont, on le verra, impénétrables l'un à

from a dialect) is its phonemic and grammatical systems and basic vocabulary, but this identity is constituted in different ways by the former, which differ at different periods but always derive as a whole from the development of the previous system of the same language (or parent language), and by the latter, which may be of any source but changes very slowly."[56] (If this is questioned on formal grounds as an unproved generalization, it is at the cost of ignoring the actual functioning of *a language* as the central means[57] in maintaining continuity of communication in a community.) A language is a whole,[58] transmitted as a whole to new speakers.[59] If "strata" may be distinguished within a language (n. 49), none the less distinct languages (unlike dialects of a language[60]) cannot be "mixed" into a new

---

l'autre", but although (p. 88) he includes the criterion "où des correspondances régulières permettent de reconnaître l'unité d'origine des mots . . .", he does not specify what category of words (for relating *languages*), and nowhere does he appear to introduce a "basic lexical fund" (which Springer and Zarechnak indeed call "this curious category") as an explicit criterion (his "fonds principal du vocabulaire courant" (p. 91), mentioned in passing as being of Germanic origin in English (cf. n. 61), is not defined in such a way as to be followed up as a general category, but appears to be an arbitrary constant (what remains Germanic only) rather than a gradually and slowly changing synchronically-defined part of any language (larger than the former may be but smaller than the total "vocabulary"), cf. Weinreich, p. 35, n. 22), and he does assert (p. 91) that "Les concordances grammaticales prouvent, et elles seules prouvent rigoureusement" – attacking American reliance on lexis, which of course M. Swadesh has since put on a time-scale basis (see R. B. Lees, "The basis of glottochronology", *Language* 29 (1953), pp. 113–27). (Professor A. S. C. Ross suggests that the mathematics of glottochronology could be disproved.)

[56] *VIIth Congress*, p. 106.
[57] Cf. L. Hjelmslev, *Omkring Sprogteoriens Grundlæggelse*, pp. 96–7.
[58] "Language is more than an aggregate of disconnected items" (Allen, p. 94).
[59] Note that this transmission, represented by Allen, p. 103, as a criterion (Meillet's) of identity, and an "extremely unsafe" "extra-linguistic" one, is in fact part of the definition of a language, spoken in the real world with its time-track (cf. Saussure, *Cours*, p. 113, on the "masse parlante"), (Allen expressly excludes time-track involving new speakers: "in terms of systematic linguistics the concept of evolutive continuity, except perhaps in the case of a biographical study, is difficult to justify".) Cf. also Smirnitsky, pp. 20–23.
[60] Cf. Meillet, *LHLG*, I, pp. 22, 30, 6.

language,[61] the language with the given strata is still identifiable as one previously existing without them.[62]

If there were exceptions to this principle, they would have to be cases of a "pidgin" formed during bilingualism,[63] but from Hall's findings it seems[64] there is no evidence of such cases occurring.[65]

If, therefore, the morphemes composing the grammar and lexical basis, or a sufficient part of them, can be traced by their "phonetic structure" (and meaning,[66] which is where grammar beyond the morphemes themselves comes in[67]) to the same origin as those of another language, the two languages must once have been one,[68] i.e. the languages themselves are genetically related. As to what constitutes a "sufficient part", each case must be judged on its merits, taking into account the conditions and extent in time[69] of the development of the given language; for example what is common to the Indo-European languages as known could not possibly have

---

[61] It is therefore incorrect for Allen (p. 91) to dismiss the question "whether English is a Germanic or a Romance language" as a "pseudo-problem". Cf. Meillet, *LHLG*, I, pp. 83, 91–2, *Introduction*, p. 36, Ross, "Probability", pp. 49, 58 (who is quite right to "rebuke" (Allen, p. 88) Anscombe and other statisticians), R. I. McDavid Jnr. reviewing L. D. Turner, *Africanisms in the Gullah dialect*, in *Language*, 26 (1950), pp. 323–33 (p. 326, n. 18).

[62] Cf. E. Haugen, "The Analysis of Linguistic Borrowing", *Language*, 26 (1950), pp. 209–31 (pp. 209–10), with references (Paul, Meillet).

[63] And logically not being itself one of the two languages of the bilingualism (that this has no cause to occur is the reason for Hall's findings in fact). This non-occurrent mixture of grammatical form-stock and lexical basis is not to be confused with the abrupt replacement of other systems (such as part of syntax, cf. n. 48) affirmed by Hall himself (*Lingua*, III, p. 145), cf. Scherer *ZIF*, LXI, pp. 211–2; Allen, p. 104; de Groot, *Lingua*, I, pp. 207–8 (A).

[64] R. A. Hall, *Lingua*, III, p. 140: all pidgins (examined) are "structurally" (cf. VII, n. 139) closer to the "base-language" (i.e. the language that is the source of the pidgin's lexical basis) than to the "native language" – so that the pidgin *is* the base-language, transformed (in adoption).

[65] On the whole question of the pidgin principle in linguistic history cf. Scherer (pp. 212, 213 and n. 5).

[66] Cf. II.

[67] Cf. VI.

[68] or "dialects" of one speech-community.

[69] according to Swadesh (cf. VII, n. 131), in the case of a section of the lexical basis (his two hundred notions) at least, extent in time only, irrespective of individual conditions. (Smirnitsky, p. 56, opposes *absolute* chronology; and cf. n. 56.)

been borrowed[70] from one to another piecemeal (i.e. sufficiently piecemeal not to violate the principle above) within the time, or in the conditions of contact, in which (however vague our knowledge otherwise) we know the languages to have existed.

Allen denies the continuous identity of languages (pp. 103–6[71]), and for justification of a "quasi-evolutive approach" demands demonstration of "an irreversibility which is (1) statable in terms of a general scheme of categories ('pandiachronic' in Sommerfelt's terminology), and (2) of a unique form such as to relate B to A rather than to any other system" (p. 104).[72] The view that such criteria do not exist is not, however, shared by all who insist on structural methods, *vide* J. Holt (*VIIth Congress*, p. 98): "If all the elements of one system determine all elements of another, such systems are two stages of the same language; but they belong to different languages if the direction of determination is shifting from one phoneme to another. The system with constants is the older one, and the stage with the variables is the younger one."[73]

To sum up I–III, we reject the implicit thesis of Allen's that:

1) comparative philology is not scientific because it is historical linguistics, for

2) historical linguistics is not scientific because it is not systemic, replacing it by the following:

1) comparative philology is not (in its material[74]) systemic be-

[70]   insofar as such material can be borrowed between languages at all, cf. nn. 42 & 55, and A. Scherer, *VIIth Congress*, pp. 503–4.

[71]   P. 105 appears to confuse panchronic irreversibility of some phonetic changes (which is not proved) with irreversibility of phonetic falling-together (the reverse of which is not merely "in basic conflict with neogrammarian principles" but "does not occur" in the real world).

[72]   Allen's gibe (at the "rebuke" referred to in n. 61) "definition of languages as brothers if and only if they were once their father" (p. 88) exposes the limitations of the "genealogical" analogy; it does not refute the fact that just as one animal couple may give rise to any number of animals, and not *vice versa*, so one language may be differentiated into any number of languages (as distinct from dialects), and not *vice versa*.

[73]   Cf. G. Bonfante, "On Reconstruction and Linguistic Method", *Word*, I (1945), pp. 83–94 (I), 132–61 (II), II, p. 159.

[74]   The *result* of comparison is of course (like the description of any state of language, cf. V (n. 103)) the establishment (in this case hypothetical) of systems. On the relation between phonemic systems and reconstruction cf. IV (n. 96).

cause what shows regularity of *development* in language is not the systems, but

2) historical linguistics (though not the comparative-philological part of it) can be systemic, and in any event

3) what is not systemic can be scientific.

IV. *The Significance and Value of Reconstructed Forms*

Allen's argument (pp. 80–84) on the question of reconstructed forms in their phonetic aspect, and of "phonemic" systems, appears to be essentially as follows. In any phonemic system, allophones can be allocated to the same phoneme only if their phonetic substance is taken into consideration. In the case of a reconstruction, "there is no substance to fall back on" ("unless we retain an extreme Schleicherian realism regarding the Ursprache and our competence to reconstruct it", p. 81) and "substantial identifications have ultimately to be made *via*" the directly observed languages (Allen: "individual languages") from which one is proceeding, which differ among themselves so that "the grouping of the asterisked allophones into asterisked phonemes may conflict with the grouping of their reflexes in individual languages, that they may conflict in varying ways in the various languages, and that as one adds new languages to the comparison so the distribution of the asterisked allophones to the asterisked phonemes may have to be altered" (p. 82).

Let us return to his argument after considering the place of the phonetic structure in the linguistic evidence for genetic relation.[75]

We have seen (in III) that whatever else changes or remains in a language, morphemes of certain types (all grammatical and some lexical) persist over long periods; moreover, that a morpheme of any type may be derived from the same source as one in another language. To this must now be added that, however irregularly or unaccountably other things in a language change (for example the gradual replacement of these morphemes by others),[76] the manner

[75] The other aspects of this evidence have been discussed in II and III.

[76] The distinction of change in phonetic units as "blind" change (as opposed to Allen's "logical necessity (p. 61), and cf. I, n. 24 from the necessarily greater

of pronouncing all these morphemes changes in a regular way,[77] in this sense, that a "sound" in a given "position" will be pronounced in the same way[78] irrespective of the particular morpheme in which it occurs, in other words speakers cannot change a "sound" in one morpheme without making the same change wherever the "sound" occurs in the same phonetic environment.

Allen denies such phonetic "laws" objective existence (pp. 61–2, cf. V) and as a difficulty in their application cites (p. 63, n. 4) their not applying "identically to morphemes of all grammatical categories without distinction". On the first point, surely Firth's words[79] on the objectiveness of system are to be taken in a diachronic way relevant here, as well as of synchronic systems. On the second, the sort of cases Allen quotes (p. 63, n. 4)[80] can be met by a sufficiently broad use of the concept of "phonetic environment" to include morphonological conditions.[81]

---

complexity of any laws of change in other linguistic units follows from the fact that what Haas refers to as "phonemic features" have no "analytic definition" (*TPS*, 1954, p. 61).

[77] Meillet, *Introduction*, pp. 26, 469–70.

[78] Cf. de Groot, *Lingua*, I, pp. 207–8: "the regularity of phonetic laws is not the result of diachronic but of synchronic laws ... A diachronic phonetic law is the formulation of the substitution of one synchronic phonetic law for another."

[79] quoted in I, reference in n. 9. Cf. "Personality and Language", p. 10: "Just as life itself is directed towards the maintenance of the general pattern of the bodily system, so also personality and language are usually maintained by the continuous and consistent activity of the bodily system, personality and language through life, language through the generations."

[80] To Allen's references we may add Meillet, *Introduction*, p. 28; Cohen, *Le Langage*, p. 60; A. S. C. Ross and R. A. Crossland, ". . . 2nd Singular for 3rd Singular", *Archivum Linguisticum*, VI (1954), pp. 112–21 (p. 120) (but cf. C. E. Bazell, "Second for Third Singular in Old Norse", *Litera*, vol. II, 1955, pp. 27–31 (p. 30)). The reason for Allen's reference to Trubetzkoy's *Das morphonologische System der russischen Sprache*, § 52, is not clear, since this work treats synchronic distinctions between morpheme-types, and the differences exemplified in § 52 are due to regular phonetic developments from IE. A good Slavonic example would have been masc. nom. *-os*, acc. *-om* > -ъ, neut. nom.-acc. *-om*, *-os* > -o (beside masc. nom. *-us*, acc. *-um*, ? neut. *-u* > -ъ).

[81] if not by *analogy* (Meillet, *Introduction*, p. 31: "loi morphologique"), e.g. Curtius' example, quoted by Allen, of *patros* not becoming *pater* like *ager* from *agros*, could be explained by analogy with other nouns of the third declension (but there is no need to perpetuate Curtius' error in deriving *patris* from *patros* not *patres*).

More serious is the question implicit in Allen's argument, what *is* a (hypothetical/"asterisked") "sound"? I.e., when we say for instance that English *t* and Latin *d*, in morphemes surviving from the one language they once were,[82] go back to (morphemes containing) one sound, how definable is this latter?

It may be sufficient answer to say that for the practical purposes of comparative philology (cf. II and V) it can be defined as that which gives rise to the sound (in these morphemes) Latin *d*, English *t*, German *z*, etc., etc.;[83] and that the symbol **d* has sufficient meaning to justify its existence if it means merely this, "that which gives rise in the given position to . . .", i.e. is merely a shorthand device.[84]

However, it is worth seeing whether there is an answer to two further questions: cannot comparative philology justify a claim[85] to *reconstruct* original forms in some degree, not merely to establish their bare existence?; and, specifically, why **d* and not **t* or any other letter occurring in the second half of the definition, or indeed any other letter or symbol at all?

To this end, we may suggest the following points of definition of an "asterisked sound":

1.a. it exists within a section of the prehistory of a language or languages
  b. this chronological situation is determined by its belonging to a section of the family covering the languages exhibiting its derivates[86]

---

[82] Cf. III, n. 68.

[83] Cf. Chikobava, pp. 197–8.

[84] Cf. Allen, pp. 72–3, p. 77 (with references): "in fact authors have variously referred to the reconstructions as 'formulaic expressions' and 'mathematical formulae'". Also L. Hjelmslev, "La stratification du langage" (Martinet, *op. cit.*, pp. 43–68), p. 44: "l'absence de substance telle qu'on la constate dans le cas d'un système construit, p. ex. en linguistique génétique ou dans un calcul typologique, à moins qu'on n'y ajoute une manifestation spécifique . . .".

[85] which we assumed in the definition and characterization of comparative philology in Introduction and II.

[86] Cf. Allen, p. 64: "We should presumably expect that different asterisked labels, with different implications, would be required according to the number and nature of the languages compared; this point, however, seems to have

c. the joint temporal and spatial extent[87] (what we may term
"section of genetic history"[88]) is progressively defined, with the

been noted by surprisingly few linguists, and the system based on a particular
chosen group of languages has been crystallized into *the* Indo-European system"
and p. 76: "Hermann provides an extreme example when considering what sort of
Ursprache we might reconstruct on the basis of only Celtic, Germanic, Balto-
Slavonic, and Albanian: then, comparing this reconstruction with the traditional
one, based on the full range of IE then known, he comes to the conclusion that
the former reconstruction was in fact 'false'." (Of course Hermann was right to
say "false", because the given languages did not form a real "section of genetic
history" (l.c. and n. 88 below), and in any case not the most comprehensive
possible one ("Ursprache").)
[87] Cf. Allen, p. 85: "the tendency for grammatically congruent phonological
statements to have a certain diachronic and diatopic extension".
[88] usually regarded from the quasi-spatial point of view as "branches" (and
other degrees of ramification, cf. VII, n. 131) within the family; for a temporal
formulation cf. G. Piccoli, *VIIth Congress*, p. 99: Ad esempio, la fase lat. *focus* . . .
è più recente della fase egualmente lat. *ignis* . . . la quale si riscontra nell' ind.
ant. . . . , nel lit. . . . e nel bulg. . . ."; Meillet, Introduction, p. 17: "Une grammaire
comparée est un système de rapports entre une langue initiale et des langues
postérieures. Poser une grammaire comparée, c'est confronter des étapes successifs, décrits aussi précisément qu'il est possible, d'une langue qui s'est differenciée
avec le temps de manière à présenter des types divers"; and in general Cohen,
Le Langage, p. 61: "L'indo-européen commun ainsi reconstitué partiellement
par inférences permet une vue hypothétique sur une période qui est pour nous
préhistorique. D'autre part, on reconstitue par la comparaison des langues
germaniques un germanique commun non attesté, etc., ces langues communes ou
masses dialectales plus ou moins unifiées étant supposées sensiblement contem-
poraines des plus anciennes langues effectivement attestées, comme le sanskrit
et le grec; en somme, on s'efforce de combler les lacunes dans la période historique", and Ross, "Probability", pp. 26–7, and Hoenigswald, p. 359, n. 2. And
while Allen is justified (subject to VII, n. 134) in emphasizing (p. 66, n. 3) "Sapir's
warning that, '. . . the concept of "a linguistic stock" is never definitive in an
exclusive sense'.", this cannot be used, as Allen appears to use it, to oppose
distinctions *within* the "stock", when he dismisses as mere "constructs" the
sections of genetic history distinguished by Sturtevant to accommodate Hittite
(however much we might agree with his attitude (p. 66) to Sturtevant's "sister-
hood" and "cousin"): "For the 'comparison of the Indo-European languages
with Hittite' Sturtevant has recourse to two additional constructs, 'Anatolian'
and 'Indo-Hittite'" (p. 65, n. 1). In fact (since the real linguistic states represented
by these sections of genetic history could never be supposed to be free of dialectal
variation, cf. III (and Smirnitsky, p. 21, Thieme, pp. 604-5)), the current rejection
of "Indo-Hittite" appears to be really only a terminological issue, as witness T.
Burrow's "more satisfactory to speak of Early and Late Indo-European, rather
than of Indo-Hittite and Indo-European" (*The Sanskrit Language*, London,
1955, p. 17). Of course, if one assumed with R. A. Crossland that the peculiarities

utilization of more and more evidence (cf. II)[89]

2.a. it is itself a "progressively defined section" – of the total range of phonetic possibilities or "articulatory spectrum" (Allen, "Phonetics", p. 136) – (and it is in this progressive definition[90] that it differs from a non-asterisked sound)

b. as a complex of features of articulation which are terms in independent systems,[91] it is defined by the dimensions (within the "total range of phonetic possibilities") on which it can be located by the abstraction of features of articulation common to the "sounds" (directly observed or themselves – in "dead" languages – "reconstructed" from written and comparative evidence) derived (according to the hypothesis) from it[92]

3.a. it does not *need* to be joined (as an allophone) in a phoneme with such sections ("complexes") in other positions (nor as a phoneme in an archiphoneme, see n. 96).[93]

b. this happens to be in accordance with the kind of (synchronic) phonology advocated by Allen[94] for ordinary (non-asterisked)

---

of Hittite (Anatolian generally) were innovations (e.g. the *loss* of the feminine) due to language-mixture (cf. III, nn. 63–5), then there *is* a difference of substance.

To be sure, the last word is far from having been said on the ordering, demarcation and general "progressive definition" of such sections, cf. II, n. 37 (and Allen, p. 87, n. 3).

[89] Cf. Smirnitsky, p. 55; V (n. 108).

[90] And not in the total absence of "substance" as in Hjelmslev quoted in n. 84.

[91] Cf. Allen, "Phonetics", p. 133, also J. Whatmough, *VIIth Congress*, p. 145.

[92] Cf. Smirnitsky, pp. 52, 31.

[93] Despite the tendency to mistake for phonemic identity the identity of letters used in different positions (which do it is true most often represent the same complex of features); cf. with Allen's "the Roman and romanized orthographies of much of the comparative material were already all but phonemic, so that little work upon them was necessary in order to make a beginning, but only a study, as Hjelmslev has pointed out, of *literarum permutationes*." (pp. 60–1), Meillet, *Introduction*, p. 464, on "phonetics" as early as Schleicher: "comme l'étude en repose sur une observation directe de la langue parlée, et non sur l'examen des vieux textes, elle porte, innovation décisive, sur l'articulation et les changements d'articulation, non sur les lettres et les correspondances de lettres d'une langue à l'autre".

[94] Allen, p. 84: "there is a current and growing tendency to move away from the traditionally phonemic type of analysis in the direction of analyses having two outstanding characteristics: (1) they are 'prosodic' in the sense that they are orientated with a view to syntagmatic implications rather than segmental

systems (and lends support to this advocacy[95]).[96]

4. it is represented (in existing practice) by a letter which in one or
    more of the derived languages (or in a language or translitera-
    tion using that alphabet – usually the Roman) represents a
    similar complex of features, or where necessary by a modifi-
    cation of such a letter.[97]

It might be difficult to formulate (for the conventions of existing
practice) how similar the complex in point 4 has to be (or to remain
[as regards our knowledge or hypotheses], for the letter not to be
replaced), but it clearly has to do with the total system within which
it is found, and, while the particular "sounds" or combinations of

---

oppositions, and so are concerned not with *literarum permutationes* but rather
with *compositio vocis*; (2) They are 'phonological', in the sense that their systems
are relevant to the structural positions for which they are established, and are
congruent with other levels of analysis, notably the grammatical". (It is not clear
how (2) differs from phonematic phonology, cf. n. 96).

[95] Cf. Allen, pp. 84–5: "This does not raise any special new difficulties for
comparison – more likely the reverse; for the categories established by these
techniques often show a wider range of application than the traditional phonemic
classes, and one can already see the possibility of their producing a greater
number of one-to-one correspondences in comparative work".

[96] It is remarkable that while, as Allen points out (p. 60: "we in fact owe the
term 'phoneme' to Kruszewski's comparative-historical studies of morphemic
alternation"), phonology (in the synchronic sense) originated in historical work
(helping to effect through the Baudouin de Courtenay school the transition to
Saussurean synchronicism), the new aphonematic ("prosodic") phonology of the
Firth school has been developed in purely synchronic work. Since its differences
from Trubetzkoyan phonology in content (as distinct from formulation) appear
to lie in more abstract categorization of the substance, the necessity of the innovation is more pressing for hypothetical-historical purposes; and Allen is to be
heartily thanked for linking the two subjects (p. 84, pp. 95–6; "Phonetics",
pp. 131–2).
(The Trubetzkoyan archiphoneme supposes that despite the different total
of alternants in different positions (e.g. in German, final (or non-pre-vowel/-
liquid) only *t*, *f*, etc., beside *t*, *d*, *f*, *v*, etc. elsewhere) it *is* possible (cf. VI, n. 127,
on terms in grammatical systems) to equate units among a lower total (e.g. *t*
(archiphoneme *T*) in *tot*, *Tod*) with pairs among a higher total (*toter*, *Todes*); the
Trubetzkoyan demarcation of phonemes could not sacrifice substantial identity
to positional function as T. Hill's aphonematic analysis of German does in
separating pre-vocalic (or final) /ʃ/ from /ʃ/ elsewhere to fill the gap *sk*.)
[97] e.g. *k* or *q* for the voiceless velar, *k̑* for the voiceless palato-velar.

features change, there is continuity in the total distinctions of features in the larger unit (syllable, word . . . – cf. II, at n. 29),[98] limiting the range of what has to be differently represented at each stage.[99]

This then is one answer to Allen's argument referred to at the beginning of this section. In phonematic terms, of course, the answer is the well-known fact that it is not phonemes that suffer atomistic change but allophones (causing the very redistribution of allophones in phonemes, or changed phonemes,[100] that Allen adduces as if unreal seeming). But Allen's own preferred terms themselves provide a more positive answer: the very fact that phonemes have only synchronic "existence" could be a reason for dispensing with them as a contribution to the re-synthesis of synchronic and diachronic advocated in I.

V. *Linguistics as a Science*

"In science", declares Allen "linguistic science included, one is not interested in 'establishing reality'" (p. 65, n. 1; cf. IV on Sturtevant).

What then *is* science according to Allen? We gather that science "in a contemporary sense" (p. 54; cf. n. 2) is to be identified with the kind of principles to be found in certain current works on the sciences (referred to at p. 52, n. 1, p. 57, n. 2, and p. 54, n. 2), principles which, it must be said, are associated with one particular kind of current philosophical views. This is not the place to discuss at

[98] Allen is right ("Phonetics", pp. 135–6) that the distinctions of feature or prosody (as opposed to their realization) are in general maintained (e.g. the Old High German inter-syllabic *i*/*j*-prosody that it maintained in later German as *umlaut* of the vowel of the first syllable, or the labial feature of the **w* in **gelw-* that is maintained in German *gelb* (or English /jelou/)); the exception is when there is *loss* (e.g. of the OHG distinction of vowels in unstressed syllables, other than that between *i*/"*j*+" and the rest, or of the distinction between stop and non-stop (semivowel/fricative) voiced labial after liquid in *gelb-* (or between unstressed vowels in vulgar English /jelə/)): there is *no new creation* of phonetic features as such, only morphological renewal – in this sense (a commonplace of historical linguistics) there *is* phonetic (phonological) "entropy" (Allen, p. 105).

[99] Allen, "Phonetics", p. 136: "more stable processes . . . features whereby the continuum of utterance is maintained"; cf. III on the continuity of language.

[100] Cf. Hoenigswald, p. 364; C. E. Bazell, "The Choice of Criteria in Structural Linguistics", *Word*, 10 (1954), pp. 126–35 (p. 133).

length the general philosophical and methodological issues posed by the various schools loosely known as "logical positivism". What one can state is that whatever else science is, it should as a minimum continue the procedures on which are based the achievements of scientific advance to date.

These would be generally agreed to include: preliminary *observation* of the evidence, with as much *systematization* of it as possible, construction of *hypotheses* that would explain the facts so far known, attempted *prediction* of new facts and checking of these by observation (including experiment where possible) in order to test the hypotheses, elaboration of the hypotheses into *theory* on this basis (interplay of systematic explanation and observation), and *use* of the theory's power of prediction for practical purposes (along with continued checking by observation).

The *observation* with which linguistics begins is observation of phenomena which are "natural phenomena" only to the extent that the material of the social sciences is, but are like the material of the natural sciences in that some of them are, some within a limited period, to be observed repeatedly. In this respect linguistics has the scope of both kinds of science.[101]

These phenomena that are observed as language are already an abstraction by *systematization* from the raw material[102] of sound heard or written marks seen, since, as Saussure put it, language is a

[101]   If, but only if, the natural and social sciences are understood as mutually exclusive, linguistics belongs to neither, language being a unique phenomenon (cf. III, and Ross: "Linguistics is apparently like nothing", "Theory", p. 2), thought it is essentially more related to the latter (e.g. the present development of linguistics [Introduction and I on intolerance of historical within scientific] is paralleled in social anthropology, vide Leach's dichotomy of historical anthropology and scientific anthropology). Cf. Scherer's distinction of linguistic levels (beside the structural distinction in IV, n. 76); "Die Lautunterschiede, die mit dem musikalischen Rhythmus des Sprechens und also letzten Endes mit der bei jedem Menschenschlag verschiedenen 'nervösen' Organisation zusammenhängen, sind also nicht Charakteristika der Sprachen, sondern der Dialekte. Sie wurzeln im Biologischen, nicht im Geistigen" (*ZIF*, LXI, p. 202).
[102]   The raw material of linguistics is that (*viz.* language) which turns the raw material of all sciences into "concepts and propositions" (Northrop, *Logic of the sciences and the humanities*, p. 36), giving it the unique "problem of the *metalanguage*" (or "language turned back on itself" – Firth, "Personality", p. 42).

system of pure values. But the further role of system in linguistic science depends, as we have seen, upon the branch of linguistics in question: while comparative philology *is* concerned with linguistic items that are apprehended as terms in systems, it is concerned with them independently of the systems,[103] whereas descriptive linguistics is concerned with the systems as such.

In all cases that much systematization is required that is demanded for the framing of *hypotheses*.[104] Such systematization is carried out according to the well-known scientific "principle of economy". Upon this principle depends the validity of the argument from cumulative probability in II.

"An hypothesis is directed towards reality."[105] That is to say that a hypothesis is tested by confronting its *predictions* with observed reality. For example, not only can comparative philology in effect "predict" retrospectively[106] forms hitherto unmet in recorded languages which are later confirmed from further records, but it also "predicted" the existence of laryngeal "phonemes" before their "reflexes" were discovered in Hittite (Allen, pp. 64–5).[107]

It is to be noted that such prediction is possible from a hypothesis which represents only one aspect abstracted from the reality with which it deals; thus it is true that the "Ursprache" of comparative-philological hypothesis is sometihng less than a "language" (cf. IV, *fin.*, and VI, *fin.*).[108] In this the science of comparative philology

---

[103] i.e. the systems of which they are now apprehended as terms, though a. not independently of possible systems reconstructed (cf. III, n. 74); b. positively, in Smirnitsky's terms (p. 45), only comparative philology makes possible, by the knowledge of where they belong, the study of items (the atoms of diachronic linguistics) as terms in (earlier) systems.

[104] *This* sense of systematization would justify Allen's equation, implied on p. 62, of science and systematization.

[105] Vaihinger, quoted by Allen, p. 76, n. 4.

[106] A concept for which L. R. Palmer has coined the term "retrodict",

[107] Cf. Bonfante, I, p. 89.

[108] Cf. Firth, ("Personality", p. 39, and) *Lingua*, I, p. 401: "Technically speaking, a 'phonetic system' is a contradiction in terms, unless it be thought that a system of notation such as that of the International Phonetic Association, purporting to represent all the typical language sounds of man, is a 'linguistic system.' Have contemporary theories of Indo-European phonology reached a similar stage? That is, do they constitute a system for a language, or type of language, or for hundreds of languages? There is nothing new in the question. 'Indo-European'

may be compared with atomic physics, which uses abstract "pic-
tures" of atomic structure to predict physical effects; but there is no
apparent limit to the process of increasing our knowledge of the
atom, whereas in comparative philology, as in other historical
disciplines depending *inter alia* on the availability of records, there
are limits that no refinement of method may be able to transcend
(cf. II, n. 37). And the Hittite "reflexes" were of course *discovered*
by accident, they could not be *looked for* as for example Neptune
was once the perturbation of Uranus had been observed.

Allen admits the explanatory function of the "Ursprache" hypothesis (pp. 76–8), but continues "the yearning for this type of explanation is understandably human, but it is not a scientific require-
ment", and adds that the "Ursprache" hypothesis itself is "an extremely primitive mode of gratifying the *explicandi cacoethes*". This
ignoring of the predictive power of such a hypothesis as a criterion
of its scientificness is characteristic of Allen's conception of science
and of the role of *theory* in the various kinds of linguistics.

Now it will be noted that Allen uses the term "*theory*" in a sense
("the Hjelmslevian sense", p. 53) different from that of normal
English scientific usage. In this terminology, which Allen has
imported from a translation (Hjelmslev's own) of Hjelmslev's
Danish, "on the basis of a theory and its theorems we may construct hypotheses (including the so-called laws), the fate of which,
contrary to that of the theory itself, depends exclusively on verification" (p. 53).

The conception of science implied in this passage may be appropriate to certain aspects of mathematics,[109] but whatever else it is

---

is not a language, any more than the International Phonetic Association Alphabet
is the alphabet of a language". Cf. Allen, pp. 72–3, 87. But the adequacy of this
"system" for the purposes of genetic linguistics is made clear by Marcel Cohen:
"Ainsi de proche en proche on a reconstitué le système phonologique hypothétique
de l'indo-européen. A vrai dire, celui-ci n'est pas pour nous une langue com-
plète et une, mais un 'système de correspondances' qui peut se rapporter à un
ensemble de dialectes n'ayant jamais connu d'unification. Mais c'est suffisant
pour définir l'ensemble dit famille indo-européenne, par contraste avec d'autres",
Le langage, p. 60. Cf. also Smirnitsky, pp. 51, 55.
[109] As raising "merely questions of logical consistency", Northrop, *op. cit.*, p. 19.

mathematics is a tool of the other sciences,[110] not a model for them.[111]

Let us see how this applies to linguistics. Having indicated on p. 55 that "general linguistics" conforms with the principles of "theory" in the Hjelmslevian sense in that a "theory" makes "only one hypothesis, namely that statements made in accordance with it will permit of an ultimate 'renewal of connection' with the material" (p. 53) "as applied in linguistics by Professor J. R. Firth" (n. 4), Allen states, p. 54, that "traditional doctrines", i.e. comparative philology, "are mainly hypothetical and not theoretical", and therefore his "theory" will not conflict with them: "where they are criticized the criticism will be directed mainly to a demonstration of this fact; they will be rejected only in so far as they claim to be scientific in a contemporary sense or to be part of General Linguistics – to belong, in fact, to the linguistic science of the twentieth century."

Here in essence we have a contrasting of "general linguistics", as practised e.g. by J. R. Firth, with comparative philology (an "antinomy" dealt with generally already in I above), the implication that the former is theoretical, and the statement that the latter is mainly hypothetical.

It is clear enough that Firth's methods permit of an ultimate renewal of connection with the material. It is not clear from Allen's exposition how they (as opposed to Allen's implicit interpretation of them in the course of his argument) conflict with comparative philology.

And in whatever other ways they differ, general linguistics (in any sense that has anything to do with real languages[112]) and comparative philology in fact both alike make use of both theory and hypotheses.

---

[110] At this point we may note that the hypotheses of glottochronometry (cf. references in III, n. 55 and VII, n. 131) if found true would constitute a "mathematical" theory of comparative philology in the sense of mathematics providing a tool really adapted to comparative philology (more so than the "statistical studies" referred to by Allen, p. 66).

[111] and linguistics is an "empirical science" (Reichling, *Lingua*, I; Robins, *Language*, p. 298).

[112] Cf. n. 111 and Reichling in VII, n. 132.

As to the theory of comparative philology, an attempt at an exposition of it was given above in II–IV. It exists even if a given comparative philologist is not consciously aware of it (cf. Allen, p. 57, n. 2) and even though the exposition of it is in great need of further refining,[113] and one may concede to this part of Allen's views the justice of his demand for more theoretical clarity (c. p. 57; cf. Robins, *Language*, 28, p. 298).

It exists because theory is not something entirely independent of the facts, but is implicit in any scientific handling of the facts, and is subject to constant improvement in the light of them. (Cf. Gonda referred to in III, n. 38.)

Allen then divorces the questions of theory and use. Thus he appears to relegate the content of comparative philology to a pragmatical region when he says: "It may again be emphasized that one does not wish to criticize the selection of criteria for the practical identification of languages by groups, as has been done for Bantu, and by Trubetzkoy for Indo-european" (pp. 91–2). Cf. his comments on the "usefulness" of sound-laws.[114]

It may be argued that *use* is one of the respects in which descriptive linguistics is superior to comparative philology, because the uses of descriptive linguistics are obviously so immediate. But the uses of comparative philology are so manifold that descriptive linguistics itself could not dispense with the existence of it (as Allen admits on p. 54), any more than the true application of comparative philology can dispense with descriptive linguistics.

The integrated application of these two kinds of linguistics will be pursued in VII. It is enough to note here that there is this much element of truth in the terminological proposal of Allen's rejected in II, n. 25, that comparative philology is of "practical" use outside linguistics itself not only in establishing the relationship of lan-

[113] Bonfante, II, p. 149: "little theoretical work", with references.
[114] pp. 61–2: "It would appear that the regularity of the 'sound-laws' was not so much a blind as a logical necessity. Yet we know that there has in the past been long and bitter controversy on this point, leading, however, in the case of the more discerning of the opposition to a recognition of the 'practical value' of such laws, and of the utter necessity of them if any systematization was to be made, in fact if the subject was to be in any way scientific . . ."

guages (and thereby aiding non-linguistic historical researches) but in helping to illuminate the usage of linguistic items[115] and thereby aiding the interpretation of (non-living) texts.[116]

VI. *Comparative Descriptive Linguistics and Allen's Proposals*

It is refreshing to turn to Allen on comparative linguistics other than comparative philology.[117]

Such comparative linguistics is of course implicit in any work on language involving a language *of* description different from that *under* description.[118] But it would not be true to say, as does Chikobava (p. 137, n.), that "Comparison of unrelated languages has significance only for the method of teaching a foreign language".[119] Comparison can be made of any two languages, for a variety of purposes.

The purpose may be the theoretical linguistics of a given language (foreign or one's own), and the language of comparison some other

[115] With the proviso made in II, n. 37, that the particular methods still ob-taining in the subject may need overhauling; on this particular application cf. (with Allen's pp. 58–60) P. J. Wexler's review of Kronasser's *Handbuch der Semasiologie*, in *Archivum linguisticum*, VI (1954), pp. 55–57 (esp. p. 56): "There are clearly a number of methodological objections to a classification based so lar-gely on an abstract psychology . . ." and E. Benveniste, "Problèmes sémantiques de la reconstruction", Martinet, *op. cit.*, pp. 31–44, and cf. VI, *fin.*

[116] Cf. F. Saran, *Das Übersetzen aus dem Mittelhochdeutschen* (Halle, 1st ed. 1930), pp. 7–8 and examples like *reine*, where the MHG meaning, lost in Modern [standard] German *rein*, "fine (as opposed to coarse)" is supported from the etymon with the supposed meaning "sift"; and (on finding meaning synchronic-ally by linguistic contexts) M. Joos and F. R. Whitesell: "it is not at all a circular argument, but rather a quite respectable accumulation of probabilities (all semantic study deals with probabilities, in contrast to grammar, where absolutes are the rule)", *MHG Courtly Reader* (Wisconsin, 1951), p. 282.

[117] Seeing that we possess in English the term "comparative philology" for the study of genetic relations (II, n. 25), it would indeed be convenient to restrict the use of the term "comparative linguistics" to naming a wider discipline of which (within the postulated unity [I, VII] of Linguistics as a whole) comparative philology would form part (VII).

[118] And therefore of course, as Allen indicates (p. 58), in the work of meaning-giving that forms part of comparative philological procedure; cf. below on grammatical meaning.

[119] Even if this is taken in the widest possible sense – to include any study of a foreign language using one's native language – (and indeed Chikobava himself makes the admission quoted below, n. 125).

language not one's own, e.g. it is in some ways more instructive (e.g. for an English speaker) to compare the word-order of Modern German with that of Chinese (or any language with similar prin- ciples of word-order) than with that of English.[120] Note that here it is a question of comparing one aspect of the languages; if other aspects are compared, it will be a matter of convenience, in a given course of study, to use the same language of comparison for each aspect, if possible.[121]

Or the purpose may be the study of two languages as confronted e.g. in the practical task of translating from either into the other. Here *all* aspects of the same languages must be covered, but the material is perforce akin to that used for the previous purpose, since one essential way of showing differences e.g. between German and Chinese word-order is parallel analysis of a text in both languages, in one of which at least it will be a translation.[122]

A particular case that may be referred to at this point is the study of successive states[123] of "the same language" not or not only for comparative-philological purposes, because they are the same language (i.e. identity of continuity – III) but for "philological" purposes (cf. II, n. 25) because successive periods of "the same

[120] If we first mark minimum units occuring in the same order as in the other language by putting Arabic numerals before them, and then *within* these units mark with capital letters the maximum units within which occur in the same order the minimum units that can be said to correspond; then comparison with Chinese gives, e.g., "1F Alles, BE was A ich später D sagen C werde, 2G bin A ich C erst B allmählich DF and E ihnen G gewahr geworden", beside comparison with English: "1 Alles, 2 was 3 ich 4C später B sagen A werde, 5B bin A ich 6D erst allmählich C an ihnen B gewahr A geworden". (The former type of specimen, together with the Chinese equivalent "reflexly" marked, illustrates most graphi- cally what H. Glinz terms the "tension" between German word-order and syn- tactical relations (*Die Innere Form des Deutschen*, Berne, 1952, p. 142).)

[121] As it is possible, e.g., to compare German semantic categories with Chinese. Cf. C. Haag, "Ausdruck der Denkordnung im Chinesischen", *Wörter und Sachen*, Neue Folge, III. 1940, pp. 1–25; "Ausdruck der Denkordnung im Deutschen", *ibid.*, IV, 1941–2, pp. 1–17. (On grammatical categories, my "On Comparative Descriptive Linguistics", *Studia Mladenov*, Sofia, 1957 [Appen- dix G].)

[122] Thus the text in n. 120 is from H. von Hofmannsthal's "Deutsche Erzähler", compared with the translation by Feng Chih (and with an *ad hoc* translation into English).

[123] Cf. Allen, p. 101 with n. 4.

literature" are written in them. For example, a practical Historical Syntax say of German will have the task of describing how the syntax of OHG, MHG, ENHG and NHG (etc.) is the same and how different, to economize, as it were, the linguistic work of the student of texts.

Or the purpose may be the ultimate comparison of an indefinite number of languages with the object of drawing conclusions about language in general. This indeed is the only way of achieving a "general linguistics" in sense 2a in I;[124] and has been much talked about[125] but is far from realization at present. Here too comparison must begin pair by pair; how far it will remain so would require to be considered in the light of Allen's proposals.

Or finally comparison may have the purpose of trying out methods of comparison, and this, given the importance of comparison for the purposes already outlined, appears to be the next task of comparative linguistics, on the basis of Allen's proposals.

These proposals start out from Allen's assertion that comparison should be not of languages but of systems within languages, and for the non-comparative-philological purposes of this section (e.g. the comparison mentioned above of *systems* of word-order) the acceptability of this as the method of "comparison of linguistic systems in terms of general linguistic criteria" is evident. "The primary object of such comparison" he continues "is to reduce the stock of categories by the erection of more general systems than those established for the single languages. The criterion of relationship will thus be

---

[124] Beyond of course the generally applicable *techniques* already achieved.

[125] Cf. the references at Allen, pp. 88–9nn. (and p. 96, n. 6), and Reichling, *Lingua*, I, p. 16: "general linguistics must necessarily include comparison of languages"; "To arrive at an adequate definition of a category in its widest sense the linguistician combines a minute analysis of a language which he commands like his native tongue with a detailed study of comparative linguistics" (*ibid.*, p. 8); "the tracing and finding of the universal categories in speech by induction lays the foundation for perfectly justified conclusions about the existence of a systematization that is common to all languages" (*ibid.*, p. 19); see also A. H. Basson and D. J. O'Connor, "Language and Philosophy (Some Suggestions for an Empirical Approach)", *Philosophy*, XXII (1947), pp. 49–65; and Chikobava: "the more languages are studied scientifically the more material will result for generalization, and the richer general linguistics will be in content", *Vvedenie v Yazykoznanie*, Pt 1 (Moscow, 1952), p. 14.

linked to the process of reduction. In fact, if there is any reduction of categories, then we shall speak of the compared systems as related: only to this extent will it be necessary to admit relationship as a yes-or-no function.[126] Relationship once established, various degrees of relationship may be determined: suppose, for example, a system A and a system B, each of 30 terms, such that a generic system *AB may be set up subsuming all the terms of A and B by a set of 35 correspondences: then the reduction will be one of 25 terms, i.e. $30 + 30 - 35$" (p. 90).

This has an evident resemblance, to revert to one example above, to the procedure that would be adopted as its framework of exposition by a systematic, descriptive but economical, Historical Syntax, namely setting up the fewest categories that will account for all stages under description. Allen's great merit is to have outlined a technique of applying with mathematical precision (cf. his pp. 92–3) this kind of comparison to comparable systems in any language.

The question remains of identifying systems as comparable, and terms within them as identical between two languages. Examples given by Allen are phonological systems with terms identified by substance ("no more objectionable than the substantial descriptive identification of allophones", p. 96), systems of lexical classes with the classes identified by semantic function, "perhaps with special reference to certain features of relevant objects in a context of situation", and grammatical systems, with the terms identified by nongrammatical function, e.g. the function of pronouns "in indicating such contextual features as relative status of speaker and hearer, inclusion and exclusion of the hearer or a third person, and so on". As to cases where the identificatory function would also be grammatical, he concludes (p. 100) that "we do not as yet possess any acceptable linguistic technique for such identification; however, we should perhaps not exclude it *a priori* as an ultimate possibility". And M. A. K. Halliday has developed what Allen says at p. 94 to the point of showing the actual possibility of comparing gramma-

---

[126] As indicated in Introduction, n. 2, we should prefer "correspondence of systems" for Allen's "relationship (of systems)"; and for his "correspondence", "correspondence (or identity) of terms".

tical terms in themselves not identifiable except grammatically, by the non-grammatical identification (ultimately by context of situation, as required by Allen) of the totality, piece by piece, of their linguistic context; e.g. in the Pekingese and Cantonese for "one dog" in the context where Pekingese uses a "marked" auxiliary noun, since the noun meaning "dog" and the numeral may be identified between the two dialects, what remains, the auxiliary noun, may be too, "if the total spread within that sub-system can be shown to be the same ... If the terms to be compared cannot themselves be definitively identified by precise contextual reference, then they may be formally related (e.g. by collocation) to other forms which can".

At this point (p. 100) Allen reverts to the question of comparative philology, saying "it is true that in traditional IE comparatism the semantic identification is generally in practice by translation: but there is the theoretical possibility of an identification *via* situational-contextual criteria". He is referring here to *lexical* "correspondences", and continues: "No such possibility seems to exist in the case of grammatical identifications ...". To the general question of the application of Allen's methods to the establishing of semantic correspondences in genetic-relating work (which we insisted in II are of relative [cumulative] significance), while we can say that the invocation of situational context appears relevant rather than the systemic mode of comparison (cf. III, *fin.*), a full answer must await the execution of the work envisaged in VII. But something must be said about the grammatical section of semantic comparison.

First, as regards genetic comparison of grammatical morphemes, we may note that since the grammatical material is better "preserved" than the lexis as a whole (III), there is a closer "mesh" giving a higher degree of probability in the individual results.

But Allen throws grave doubts on the *possibility* of comparison of grammatical morphemes for any purpose, by saying (p. 79): "Grammatical categories are set up with regard to the paradigmatic and syntagmatic inter-relationships of the forms of a particular language, and as yet no valid method has been evolved for the identification of such functions in two or more languages; certainly it is quite illegitimate to identify a category in one language with a category in another because we happen, for purposes of terminological economy, to call them both 'genitive' or 'aorist' – such terminological equations are, however, not unknown to comparative linguistics, ancient and modern. In this connection it may be noted that we identify, for example, *equus* and *aśvaḥ*, and not e.g. *equus* and *aśvam*. On the functional side, very strictly speaking, the one identification is no more or less justified than the other . . ."[127]

This could in any case be answered with sufficient application of Halliday's method outlined above; but if it is simply a question, as it is in comparative-philological work, of deciding (even "very strictly speaking") if one corresponds rather than another, without bringing in reference to situational context at all we can make a purely formal distinction by observing the linguistic contexts of the forms -*s*/-*ḥ* and -*m*, notably the fact that the verb agrees (in number) with forms that commute with -*s*/-*ḥ*, but never varies with variation of the forms that commute with -*m*.[128]

Finally, it should be clear that the fact that we *can* compare grammatical morphemes to the extent of reconstructing the form of an original morpheme and attaching some meaning to it (and a more closely defined meaning than we can to a lexical morpheme

[127] which goes further than Firth when he says ("General Linguistics", p. 85): "'meanings' [are] determined by inter-relations of the forms in the grammatical systems set up for the language. A nominative in a four case system would in this sense necessarily have a different 'meaning' from a nominative in a two case or a fourteen case system, for example." But even this does not appear necessarily true. (Cf. IV, n. 96.) It is true that a case (or any other member of a category) has a different meaning if it is one of a number of cases sharing differently (because a different number, or for any other reason) a range of possible meaning; but a nominative, for example, may be opposed to a set of other cases, and irrespective of the number in this set may still share the range in the same way, e.g. (not to mention Sanskrit, with seven other cases) Latin and Greek nominative – vocative – the rest (respectively four and three), as contrasted with e.g. either Finnish or Russian, where the complement-function is shared.

[128] If this be held not to be "purely formal" because commutation (here to establish members of the category of case as realized in the particular morphemes under consideration) implies some criterion of reference (*salva significatione*, to quote Y. Bar-Hillel's distinction of commutability within replaceability, in "Logical Syntax and Semantics", *Language*, 30, 1954, pp. 230–7), then no analysis of real language can be "purely formal".

because it belongs to a system of which more of the terms are known, cf. above) does not mean that we can reconstruct the original "grammar" to the extent of being able to form sentences as in Schleicher's fable. Thus Allen (pp. 78–9, "Phonetics", pp. 127–8) is right to the extent that there can be no "comparative grammar" in the sense of "starred sentences" – there can be starred words in starred relations,[129] but no starred contexts (at the various levels) to make them into (starred) utterances.

VII. *General Comparative Linguistics and Comparative Philology*

If now, as we have argued, general linguistics contains as branches both "comparative philology", i.e. genetic comparative linguistics, and comparative descriptive linguistics (VI), what is the relation between them, and the specific relation of each to general linguistics? Is there a general comparative linguistics providing the principles of both the above kinds of comparative linguistics? And how does comparative linguistics of any kind contribute to the principles of general linguistics?

It should first be noted that (despite Allen, p. 87, quoted in I, n. 4) while genetic comparative linguistics is certainly not "general" in sense 2 of I, that is general simply to any language (since it cannot operate purely with one language in the same way as general linguistics$_2$), it in fact is general to any language-*family*, and (less truistically) any language may belong to a family – though it is a question of availability of evidence whether in practice a given language can be assigned to any family,[130] and how wide familes can be extended.[131]

[129] Smirnitsky, p. 44: morphological categories give *some* conclusions about syntax.
[130] See sub-section (a), and cf. III, n. 38; Meillet quoted by Allen, p. 75; Allen himself, pp. 86–7.
[131] i.e. how anciently differentiated are the languages that the possible "time depth" of our methods allows to be embraced in one total genealogical operation (on families of or within families cf. IV, n. 88). "By calculating the probability of chance and by empiric study of borrowings in non-cultural vocabulary, I conclude that time-depths up to about 12,000 years can be demonstrated in favourable circumstances by present-day comparative methods", M. Swadesh, *VIIth Congress*, p. 134. Cf. E. Cross, *ibid.*, p. 96, and my criticisms of the "lexicostatistical constant", *ibid.*, p. 106, and the references to glottochronometry in II, n. 55 and V, n. 110.

(a) What is general to comparative linguistics, if anything, is general (1), not (2) which could only be general without comparative. Hence the incorrectness of the view denounced by Reichling[132] that comparative philology could develop into "general linguistics", besides the fact that its starting-point is that it ignores what a very particular case of linguistics comparative philology is.

So the answer to the question "Can there be general comparative linguistics?" is "yes" if and only if principles underlying comparative descriptive linguistics have any application in comparative philology.

Now as we have seen in VI these principles may be of help in clarifying the theory of the detailed technique of comparative-philological work to date, e.g. of IE.[133] But clearly they have no decisive part to play in such work, because families like IE are already established. (This includes their use in the comparison of successive stages of the same language as part of comparative-philological work, but that is not to deny their great importance there for more general purposes, see VI.)

Where they conceivably could play such a decisive part is in the

---

[132] *Lingua*, I, p. 10: "When, in the beginning of the nineteenth century, the comparison of languages gained its first great successes the 'generality' was understood by many to mean the study of the greatest possible number of languages according to the historical-comparative method. This was the ideal of Bopp no less than that of Benfey and Curtius. Only this generality is and was a task one can set oneself, an ideal of 'comparative' linguistics, but it cannot produce a new autonomous branch of linguistics. Wilhelm von Humboldt saw this quite clearly when he said of 'das allgemeine Sprachstudium' that this province of study 'diesen Namen führt, weil es *die Sprache im Allgemeinen* zu ergründen strebt, nicht weil es alle Sprachen umfassen will, wozu es vielmehr nur wegen jenes Zweckes genöthigt wird'." Cf. also Meillet, *LHLG*, I, p. 36.

[133] Cf. (at as it were the pre-[Allen]"scientific" stage) Ellis and Halliday, *VIIth Congress*, p. 117: "the construction of a grammar of their parent-language based not only on all the related languages (as was the Neo-Grammarian account of the Indo-European verb) but on general comparison with other languages (as is say Prokosch's account of the Indo-European verb)" (for the dubiety of this field of syntax cf. below at n. 139); S. Ullmann: "The semantic habits of races at approximately the same level of civilisation as were the speakers of the proto-glossa may give an idea of the lexical structure of the latter . . .", *ibid.*, p. 110; E. Reifler: "comparative semantics may become a valuable source of information relative to the cognacy of phonologically compatible forms", *ibid.*, p. 110, and the reference there to J. Vendryes. Also J. Holt, *ibid.*, pp. 378–9.

establishing (or the converse?[134]) of genetic relations between languages hitherto not proved to be related,[135] such as on the one hand supposed families like Indonesian where IE-like methods have not brought IE-like proof,[136] or on the other hand wider groupings like the languages of East Asia and the Islands[137] where IE-like methods are excluded (or even where they would disprove) IE-like relation).

In both these cases what is absent is large-scale (in IN sufficiently large-scale) correspondence of morphemes, what is present is correspondence of syntactical items, measurable by comparative systems on Allen-principles of comparative descriptive linguistics (VI).

---

[134] The most we can hope for in the way of *disproof* (Smirnitsky, p. 24) of genetic relation is, if glottochronometrical constants (n. 131) *can* be established, incompatibility between the known age of a language and the derivability of its relevant material from a given family; the least (and this clearly could not apply to putative families of whole families like East Asian), the consequences of the fact (III at n. 61) that a language cannot belong to more than one family (e.g. it is *provable* that English is *not* a Romance language [III, n. 61] or that relationships claimed by N. Y. Marr [cf. II, n. 34 and *op. cit.* in n. 35] such as the diverse origins of German and Gothic, are *impossible* [not only *not proved* by his "theory"] because, e.g., German and Gothic *are both* Germanic).

[135] Allen, p. 87: "On the other hand certain groups may display impressionistic similarities [cf. II, n. 37!] which, however, refuse to break down in accordance with IE comparative principles". Cf. Meillet, *Introduction*, p. 17: "Une grammaire comparée est faite dans la mesure où les états de langue successifs et divers que l'on considère sont mis en rapport définis les uns avec les autres. Jusqu'ici on n'y est bien parvenu que pour les langues indo-européennes".

[136] Gonda, *Lingua*, I, p. 89: "The smaller the number of original elements, the more difficult will be the application of our method. As a complete agreement between petrified forms only permits us to ascribe them to the parent language, a complete agreement between forms belonging to living formations, however, points at best to the originality of the type, the existence of identical derivations in a number of IN languages which have in common several living formantia and affixes does not prove their belonging to original IN. As to the original identity of certain forms and formations, appearances are deceptive, because two or more related languages may undergo parallel modifications. In the IN field, where cultural and other circumstances are to a high degree uniform and languages are often closely related, the chances are that parallel developments have, comparatively speaking, taken place on a large scale". Another point of view (*phonetic* "waste space"; cf. I, n. 24?), C. C. Berg, *VIIth Congress*, pp. 401–2.

[137] Halliday, *VIIth Congress*, pp. 96–7.

When this measurement has been carried out,[138] the question will still remain what is the significance of syntactical resemblance. It is certain that the morpheme-material part of "grammar" is an essential part of language-identity (in the sense of III); it is not yet worked out how much of the patterns of syntax is so too,[139] it is only certain that much of it can be borrowed.[140]

All that can be stated at present, but it deserves to be stated with emphasis, is the usefulness of applying Allen's methods whether or not genetic conclusions may ensue.

b) The use of comparative descriptive linguistics (or subject to (a), general comparative linguistics) to general linguistics is evident.

But, as a special case of comparative linguistics, the use of comparative philology has a special importance; and this is one reason why despite its particularity (of peculiar concreteness) comparative philology is of such irreplaceable importance in linguistics (continuingly so, in addition to its historical role in the genesis of modern linguistics).[141]

[138] in itself constituting the work of "typology" (in the ordinary sense), not opposed to but at a different level from comparative philology (with "affinité" intermediate, cf. III, n. 50); cf. Halliday: "typology is of systems". (The appearance of opposition [though avoided in Halliday's application of Allen] may result from Allen's confusing use of "relation", see Introduction, n. 2, and VI, n. 126). See also J. Holt, *VIIth Congress*, p. 379, L. Hjelmslev, *ibid.*, pp. 428–9.

[139] Cf. M. Guthrie (*VIIth Congress*, pp. 94–5) asking "whether or not structural affinity shall be introduced into comparative study. Clearly there is no *a priori* reason why it should not be, but since it is of a different order from the kind of relationship dealt with by the more usual comparison of items of vocabulary and grammatical apparatus, the two methods cannot readily be synthesized". Meillet himself (cf. III, n. 55) seems to overlook the comparative precariousness of this field as hitherto worked when he speaks of "Les bases de la syntaxe comparative" (*Introduction*, p. 477) and of "la théorie de l'emploi des formes et de la phrase" (p. 459) and says "les comparatistes inspiraient d'autant moins de confiance . . . qu'ils négligeaient la syntaxe" (p. 463).

[140] Cf. III at n. 46; *VIIth Congress*, p. 125; Gonda quoted in n. 136; Weinreich, pp. 37–43.

[141] Cf. Meillet, *Introduction*, p. 482: "on a observé maintenant un grand nombre des ces faits particuliers, au cours de l'histoire déjà longue des divers idiomes depuis l'indo européen jusqu'à l'époque moderne; à côté de la grammaire comparée des langues indo-européennes, il s'en est constitué d'autres pour le sémitique, le finno-ougrien, l'indonésien (et, d'une manière plus générale, le malayo-polynésien), le berbère, le bantou, etc. On dispose ainsi d'une vaste collection de faits, et l'on peut étudier les conditions générales de l'évolution du langage"; and p. 483.

Comparison of states of different languages will ultimately give us principles of states of languages.[142] Comparison of history of different languages irrespective of genetic relation will ultimately give us principles of history of languages.[143] But comparison of history of genetically related languages (comparative philology) tells us immediately that one and the same language[144] has come to have different histories in different conditions, and ultimately how the realization of the principles of the history of languages is affected by the different conditions (of the differentiated communities speaking the related languages). In a word, for the laws of development of "language" (languages) crucial importance reposes in the study of development of *a* language into languages.[145]

Thus comparative philology constitutes a unique and essential part of the substance of future historical-generalizing linguistics and hence of general linguistics in the fullest sense. It provides material of which this general linguistics will provide the interpretation.

[142]   cf. Reichling, following Gabelentz (ref., I, n. 9): "what . . . characteristics regularly appear together . . . theoretical reflection on these formulae derived from experience will have to demonstrate their needfulness".

[143]   Cohen, *Le Langage*, pp. 62–3: "Les évolutions internes, qui se font suivant des modes propres au langage, reflètent les événements de manières variées. On peut reconnaître un fait essentiel: en chaque endroit et en chaque période, l'héritage du passé est une donnée partielle, mais les système actuel dépend des circonstances nouvelles. Il en résulte qu'une langue peut se transformer profondément dans son esprit et que des langues d'origines différentes peuvent avoir, avec un matériel différent, une structure analogue.

"D'où la nécessité d'un comparatisme structural à côté du comparatisme généalogique. Mais ce comparatisme structural aussi doit être historique et évolutif. Il s'agira en définitive pour la linguistique de se rendre compte dans quelle mesure les fonctionnements des langues dépendent des circonstances données dans chaque société, et quel est le rapport de leurs évolutions avec les changements des ces circonstances."

[144]   Cf. III, n. 68.

[145]   · e.g. of a Germanic dialect-continuum into Dutch and German.

Appendix C

SOME PROBLEMS IN COMPARATIVE LINGUISTICS

Comparative linguistics in the widest sense is as old as linguistics itself. The origins of objective thought about language involved the confrontation of one language, or form of a language, with another. Linguistic studies in the west may be said to begin with the description of Greek for learners with another mother-tongue, or of Classical Greek for speakers of Hellenistic Greek. Similarly, while differing in being for sacred purposes, the analysis of Sanskrit made by the Ancient Indian grammarians was for those whose mother-tongue deviated from Classical Sanskrit.

Modern, or 'scientific', linguistics, dating from the turn of the 18th and 19th centuries, began as a particular comparative study of languages, usually termed in English comparative philology, or the comparative historical method. How this is distinguished from comparative linguistics in general is one of the problems of comparative linguistics that will concern us.

This comparative philology dominated the science of linguistics until the present century, when attention was redirected to the material of pre-scientific linguistic studies, the description of single languages. Contemporary general linguistics, then, owes its origin partly to the previous development of comparative philology, partly to the resuscitation of the traditions of descriptive linguists since the ancients, especially the Indians.

Now that general linguistics exists in the sense that it does, comparative philology (or any other kind of comparative linguistics) cannot be regarded as synonymous with linguistics as a whole. It has become essential to distinguish clearly between simple descriptive linguistics, the study of one language in itself, and comparative linguistics, the comparison, for some purpose, and in some way, of two or more languages. And equally to ascertain clearly how far comparison of languages is and is not possible within the scientific framework of general linguistics.

Controversy is still proceeding on this latter subject. The most recently published contribution is F. R. Palmer's comment (in his paper to the Philological Society[1] on "Comparative Statement and Ethiopian Semitic") on W. S. Allen's conception of comparative linguistics[2] and on M. A. K. Halliday's.[3] While Allen seems to wish to rid ('scientific') comparative linguistics of comparative philology, Palmer, in opposing both Allen's and Halliday's use of the term "comparative", appears to wish to exclude descriptive comparison, while attempting to reformulate the comparative historical (his "comparative") in a synchronic way. I shall return to these distinctions especially in discussing the problem of comparative philology.

My own view[4] is in general that it is possible to develop what I term general comparative linguistics, as a methodologically useful framework to contain both comparative descriptive linguistics and comparative philology (genetic comparative linguistics); and I shall here touch on a few particular problems illustrating the relations of these disciplines.

As has been indicated, comparative linguistics, even general comparative linguistics, is only one part of general linguistics. But it is an essential part, a fact not always appreciated theoretically in discussion of general linguistics. (For example, C. E. Hockett's *Course in Modern Linguistics*,[5] which devotes appreciable space to comparative philology, and makes some sporadic references to particular descriptive comparisons, has no section on comparative descriptive linguistics as such[6] or general comparative linguistics.)

[1] *Transactions*, 1958, pp. 119–143, especially pp. 122–4.
[2] "Relationship in Comparative Linguistics", *TPS*, 1953, pp. 52–108.
[3] "Some aspects of systematic description and comparison in grammatical analysis", *Studies in Linguistic Analysis* (Special Volume of Philological Society) (Oxford, 1957), pp. 54–67.
[4] "General Linguistics and Comparative Philology", *Lingua*, VII (1958), pp. 134–174 [Appendix B].
[5] New York, 1958.
[6] Chapter 31, "The Grammatical Core" (31.1 "Comparing Grammatical Systems") offers no awareness of the problems Allen and Halliday ventilate.

The term "general linguistics" is also used for the branch of linguistics dealing with any one language descriptively; and something needs to be said about this descriptive linguistics before treating comparative descriptive linguistics. What distinguishes modern scientific descriptive linguistics is that it analyses language rigorously in terms of itself, not of something exterior to it such as thought, or logic,[7] or 'meaning' other than the uses of utterances themselves in the context of the rest of the language (and of observable situations). Its "principal aim", says W. Haas,[8] is "to describe the utterances of a language in terms of intralingual relations. Descriptive Linguistics has come to be Structural Linguistics: all elements of speech (phonological, lexical, and grammatical) are now to be defined and classified in terms of their relations to one another".

Of the various schools of descriptive linguistics in the world, particular mention must be made of the name of J. R. Firth, whose London school have developed the analysis by levels,[9] including the contextual, and on the level of phonology emphasis on prosodic units, that Allen and Palmer are attempting to apply to comparative linguistics.

Given such a structural or systemic nature of descriptive linguistics, it follows that the material to be compared by comparative descriptive linguistics will consist in systems, i.e. comparable systems in different languages. But the question arises of identifying systems as comparable, and terms within them as identical between two languages. Phonological systems present no great difficulty. But semantic systems set problems the solution of which appears to be the finding of linguistic contexts referable to an identical context of situation. Allen limits grammatical terms comparable by available methods to those where the identificatory

---

[7] H. Reichenbach's "Analysis of Conversational Language" (Chapter VII of his *Elements of Symbolic Logic*, New York, 1957) is not about "linguistics", as he implies (in criticizing grammarians), but would constitute an intermediate discipline (as now appears to be recognised in the writings of W. V. Quine).

[8] "On defining linguistic units", *TPS*, 1954, pp. 54–84 (p. 54).

[9] See now M. A. K. Halliday, "Categories of the Theory of Grammar", *Word*, 17 [and other references in Appendix A above].

function is non-grammatical (e.g. personal pronouns), but Halliday
has shown that Allen's method for comparing linguistic systems
can in fact be extended to other grammatical terms (e.g. classifiers in
Chinese dialects) by cumulative identification of components of the
linguistic context.

Now according to Palmer (p. 121), a comparative "type of statement may be regarded as differing from the descriptive analysis of a
single language only in the extent of its material". To me such a
view appears to ignore the nature of the identity and individuality
of a language. Palmer's argument is that "Even the description of
the speech of one man must be based upon generalizations from
many styles. A more general statement is required for a dialect,
and then for a language". So far the argument is sustainable in that
the difference between each dialect in a dialect-continuum and its
neighbour is negligible as far as communication is concerned; but
he continues (p. 122) "It is only a further step, though often a big
one, to the linguistic description of a pair, or a number of languages". How far this can be justified with genetically related
languages, of which alone Palmer allows what he calls comparative
treatment, needs to be considered further under the subject of
comparative philology (n. 16). But as regards general comparison
of languages, which he agrees with Allen must be by systems, he
says (p. 122) that this is no different from description of a single
language, which in Firth's terms must be polysystemic. This however appears to be a misunderstanding of Allen's point, as is his
treatment of systems in comparative philology to which we shall
come (n. 21). To say that the description of any one language
must be polysystemic means that a language consists of an agglo-
meration of systems, not a unitary system of systems, Meillet's
"système où tout se tient" (one of Firth's most notable findings is
the establishment of the principle exemplified by the work of his
pupils and others,[10] that one language (i.e. one fundamental means

[10] J. R. Firth, "Sounds and Prosodies", *TPS*, 1948, and references there; E.
Henderson, "The Phonology of Loanwords in some South-East Asian Languages", *TPS*, 1951; my "Structure of Neologisms in Russian and Czech",
unpublished London Ph.D. thesis, 1948, and Proceedings of the Seventh Inter-

of communication socially shared) may consist of diverse strata, historically of differing origin, synchronically generalizable into distinct systems, e.g. Latin words in English). But to say that the comparison of languages must be by systems means that one system in language A corresponds more to one in language B, another in language A to one in language C.

The individuality of languages, even related ones, thus apparently played down by Palmer (the Englishness of English, etc.) that is part of the point of descriptive comparison (as well as their ultimate isomorphism or essential translatability[11]) may be exemplified by the instance given in C. Rabin's "The Linguistics of Translation" in the UCL *Studies in Communication* 2, *Aspects of Translation*, 1958: "Jack sees Jill" has the same referent as "Jill is seen by Jack", "Jill is visible to Jack", "Jack's view of Jill";[12] similarly "Jack likes Jill" has the same referent as German [Rabin's 'literal' translation] "Jack has Jill gladly", Italian "Jack wishes well to Jill", Hebrew "Jill finds favour in the eyes of Jack"; "I have money" has the same referent as Hebrew, Japanese or Latin "to me there is money", Arabic or Russian "with me there is money", Turkish "my money exists". "The symbols marking the relation have no individual references at all, though the referents of the words when standing by themselves are present in the complex reality symbolized by the sentence. In 'Jack likes Jill' the situation contains the elements represented by: *gladly*, *wish*, *favour*, and *Jack's eyes*; in 'I have money' it contains those represented by: *to me*, *with me*, *have*, *there is*, and *exists*. Each language makes its own selection from the relevant elements and thereby, for the community using it, adequately symbolizes the situation as a wole".

A description of this material of the kind advocated by Palmer might be thought to come down to a mere identification of the

---

national Congress of Linguists, p. 125. On more general forms of polysystemicness cf. n. 21.

[11] For the limits of which cf. W. V. Quine, "Meaning and Translation", *On Translation*, ed. R. Brower (Cambridge, Mass., 1959), pp. 148–172.

[12] Cf. above, n. 7.

common context of situation,[13] abstracting altogether from the linguistic form. Yet even here it is possible to trace Allen's kind of correspondence between linguistic systems not related genetically, i.e. to show some similar distribution of terms of a system among different contexts, e.g. the tenses in the languages in Rabin's examples, or the English Present Continuous and Simple and the Turkish Present and Present Aorist.

I should like now to turn to the more particular case of linguistic comparison where it is a fact, or a possibility, that the languages providing the material to be compared are related in origin, and this fact or possibility matters for the comparison, i.e. constitutes the reason for or purpose of it. Since we are discussing this in its relation to general comparative linguistics, I shall not here[14] go into the question of the validity of the concept of relation by origin of whole languages, on which comparative philology rests – in my opinion quite securely, whatever queries of detail may arise. That is to say, it does seem possible (where the evidence is available, as it is for example for the Indo-European languages) by the comparison of certain kinds of linguistic items to establish the common origin of two or more languages.

To say that languages are of common origin means that once there was one language, or dialect-continuum, in the dialects[15] of which, as it passed from one generation to another, each remaining comprehensible to the other, different changes resulted finally in the speakers of one dialect not being comprehensible to the speakers of another.[16] This process is of course observable in recorded

[13]   In fact (as well as confining comparative treatment to what is genetically related) Palmer (in "Linguistic Hierarchy", *Lingua*, VII, 1958, pp. 225–241, p. 237) rejects any use of context of situation except for the distinction of different styles as being used in *different* contexts of situation ("styles, different kinds of language that are mainly determined by the kind of activity in which the speaker is engaged").

[14]   See "General Linguistics and Comparative Philology" [Appendix B].

[15]   On the role of dialect relations in the postulated development of linguistic innovation cf. Hockett, *op. cit.*, Chapter 60.

[16]   Once this has happened, and the new languages stand to each other, as far as ordinary speakers are concerned, in the same relation as any distinct languages (cf. "General Linguistics and Comparative Philology", p. 149 [Appendix B, p. 86]), Palmer's "only a further step, though often a big one" (quoted above)

history, e.g. Latin giving the Romance dialects out of which the Spanish, French, Italian, Rumanian, etc., languages have emerged. (The fact of dialect continuity between some of these remaining today confirms their origination without nullifying the distinctness of the dialects which have become standard languages.)

Now comparative philology has constructed, in part, the original forms of proto-Indo-European from which words, inflections, etc. of English, Latin and other languages can be shown to be derived, e.g. there was, it is said, a stem *patér-, giving Latin *pater* by one development (*p, t, r, e* "remain", *ə > a*, accent shifts back), English *father* by another.[17] Is this like saying that we know from texts, etc., that there was a Latin word *patrem*, which gave by one development French *père*, by another Spanish *padre*, and so on?

The reconstructed Vulgar Latin from which the Romance forms are actually to be derived, can be more or less checked from Classical Latin (as well as more directly from some more colloquial records), whereas proto-Indo-European is a pure construct. We know from various sources more or less how Latin was pronounced in its various forms. Can we say that we know how *patér-* was pronounced; do the letters *p, ə*, etc. mean anything more than *x*, which *> p, f*, etc., *y*, which *> a*, Indo-Iranian *i*, etc.? (In the words of Saussure quoted by Jakobson at the VIIIth Congress of Linguists, "One could without specifying its phonic nature catalogue

---

becomes a gulf which the linguistic analyst can bridge (by comparative descriptive linguistics) only, in principle, to the same extent as he can that between any languages.

[17]   R. A. Hall, "On Realism in Reconstruction", *Language*, 36 (1960), pp. 203–6, considers that *utterances* can be reconstructed, in proto-Indo-European as well as in proto-Romance, and that instead of discarding Schleicher's famous fable when his phonology was overhauled it should have been re-written. "We are now in a position to reconstruct not only phonemes and morphemes, but tagmemes (and hence, inevitably, texts) both for the farthest stages we can reach going backwards in time and also for intermediate periods". (p. 206). But *reconstructing* tagmemes which must have occured in utterances of the language is a different matter from fabricating whole utterances or texts (like his "Illa uilla de illas bestias", or the Schleicher fable) which have tagmemes in common with the hypothetical language but not their contexts in common with anything known of it. (Cf. "General Linguistics and Comparative Philology", p. 169 [Appendix B, p. 107].)

it and represent it by its number in the table of Indo-European phonemes".)

In fact the letters do mean something more, because it is reasonable to suppose that what gives sounds like *p*, *f*, etc., which have in common such features as labiality, must itself have had these features,[18] just as the stem must have meant something connected with the meanings like "father" that the words have.[19]

This identification of phonetic features in a given position in the word rather than of phonemes summing up allophones at various positions coincides with the prosodic method of the Firth school in synchronic linguistics.

The prosodic treatment of genetic history has been translated by Palmer into purely synchronic statements of common morphemes for grammatical categories (or presumably lexical items[20]) in two or more languages. To restrict one's statement of genetic relation to this, without reconstructing, as far as possible (and taking account of analogical replacement), the systems at all levels of the

[18] To arrive at the feature of plosiveness absent from the Germanic *f* (or that of voice in IE*d, absent from the Germanic *t*), it was necessary to infer (is necessary to invoke) the Germanic Consonant-Shift as a whole, and in relation to the consonant-reflexes as a whole of the other extant IE languages as a whole; this is but an extreme example of the need to consider whole systems, and all relevant languages.

[19] For things that we do *not* know about such original linguistic items cf. N. E. Collinge, "Laryngeals and Indo-European Ablaut and Problems of the Zero Grade", *Archivum Linguisticum*, V (1953), pp. 75–87. The formulation by 'features' of our knowledge or hypotheses at a given stage will in fact facilitate transition to a stage of more detailed knowledge or knowledge of an earlier stage, e.g. the laryngeal 'stage' of IE phonetics; thus derivation of *ə from zero-grade of syllable containing laryngeal consonant would be formulable as combination of features of absence of normal vowel and presence of laryngeality of given kind. (Cf. "General Linguistics and Comparative Philology", pp. 157–8 [Appendix B, pp. 94–95] (and n. 98)[).

[20] "Comparative Statement" pp. 122–4 (". . . an appeal to meaning may be necessary in dealing with lexical elements, but can be avoided in the grammatical statement. The only basis for the identification of the grammatical elements is a formal one – that it makes a single formulaic statement possible".) In general, his distinction of levels is obscured, partly by his use of the term 'phonology' (p. 126: "Phonology in this sense includes much that is usually handled in morphology"). (Cf. also "Linguistic Hierarchy".) For a clear treatment of levels, including 'form', see Halliday, "Categories . . .".

original language, seems to me an impoverishment of the method.

This is not to say that Palmer's modes of comparative statement could not be put to positive use. Refinements of method would also be one positive result of Allen's critique of comparative philology. One of them is the clarification of the relation of the different kinds of comparative linguistics to the systemicness of linguistic material.[21]

In descriptive linguistics, and therefore in comparative descriptive linguistics, one is concerned with linguistic units as terms in systems; that is their definition. In comparative philology the material to be compared, once identified, consists in items irrespective of the systems they constitute in the extant languages, though

[21] Cf. "General Linguistics and Comparative Philology", pp. 151, 160 [Appendix B, pp. 88, 97].

In setting up his alternative formulation to traditional comparative philology, Palmer has this to say about the question of system and comparative linguistics (pp. 122–3): "Different phonological statements may be required, for instance, for the verbal and nominal forms of a language, or even for the stems and endings of morphologically related words. But for each *system* of this type a full linguistic investigation is required, with statements at various levels of analysis, and, indeed, resting upon the recognition of the congruence and inter-dependence of these levels. But the systems to which Allen refers do not appear to be systems in this sense. For one example of the systems that he suggests might be compared are two systems of pronouns with a specific denial that there is any phonological identity of the pronominal forms. Another is a set of systems of lexical classes, with again no parallelism at the phonological level. But this type of statement is not comparative in the sense in which the term is used here. For in any kind of linguistic statement, whether comparative or not, the recognition of the interdependence of levels is an essential characteristic, and a comparative statement, no less than the statement for a single language, must involve analysis at the various levels". (The assumption that the linguistic analysis of one language (for which the interdependence of levels *is* essential) must be the model (in a mechanical way) for all linguistics is reminiscent of Allen's treatment of (general) linguistics as synonymous with descriptive linguistics, see "General Linguistics and Comparative Philology", especially pp. 136–7 [Appendix B, pp. 73–74].)

But this only amounts to saying that in related languages, or more precisely for the present purpose, in the genetically related *parts* of any languages, there is a common relation between the different levels, what he quotes Allen as calling "distributional-semantic" phonemic comparison, but in non-related ones an independent relation in each case, e.g. the meaning 'father' at the semantic level in both English and Latin is related to a labial consonant, etc., at the phonological level, etc., but in non-Indo-European languages is not.

It seems to me a violation of the normal usage of "comparative" to confine it to this kind of case and for other comparison to use (as he does, pp. 124–5) "typology" (widening the meaning of that term). (Is typology then not linguistics?)

the end-result may be the hypothetical construction of the systems constituted by the original units that have developed into this material.

For example, the complex problem of the initial mutations in Celtic languages takes on different aspects according as one is making a descriptive statement or reconstructing origins. What in Modern Welsh constitutes a term in a system of alternations, e.g. apical voiceless stop – fricative – voiced (stop) – nasal (voiceless), is turned into a hypothetical proto-Celtic sound, e.g. apical voiceless stop, in various phonetic environments.

To pursue this example in some detail will help to illustrate the demarcations and possible interrelations of descriptive linguistics, comparative descriptive linguistics, and genetic comparative linguistics.

A descriptive statement of the initial mutations in Welsh will have to begin from the occurrences of particular variations of particular initial sounds in their contexts. It seems possible to group these into nine sets, which may be termed 'functional series' to distinguish them from the phonological groupings abstracted from the contexts (below):

1.	p	t	c	b	d	g	m	ll	rh	–
2.	p	t	c	b	d	g	m	ll	rh	h
3.	ph	th	ch	b	d	g	m	ll	rh	h
4.	ph	th	ch	b	d	g	m	ll	rh	–
5.	ph	th	ch	f	dd	–	f	l	r	–
6.	b	d	g	f	dd	–	f	l	r	–
7.	b	d	g	f	dd	–	f	ll	rh	–
8.	b	d	g	b	d	g	m	ll	rh	–
9.	mh	nh	ngh	m	n	ng	m	ll	rh	–

Other initials, e.g. n–, s–, are the same in all nine.

The contexts of occurrence of the nine are:

1. word in isolation,[22] and in other contexts other than 2.–9., e.g. *eich tad,* 'your father', *yn gweled pobl,* 'seeing people'.

[22] i.e. quoted as word (forming a one-word sentence, on the other hand, it may show variation, e.g. "dad!", "'nhad!") – this observable evidence of the speaker's

2. after certain possessive pronomina forms, e.g. *ein, 'm*.
3. after certain possessive pronominal forms, e.g. *ei*, 'her'.
4. after certain words, viz., *a*, 'and', *â, na* ('than'), *gyda, tra, tua, tri, chwe*.
5. after certain words, viz., *oni, ni, na* (negative).
6. after certain words, viz., *a* interrogative, *pa, a* and *na* relative, *pan, fe, mi, dy/'th, ei/'i/'w* ('his'), *dyma, dyna, dacw, go, rhy, am, ar, at, dan, dros, gan, heb, hyd, i, o, trwy, wrth, neu, dau, ail, ychydig, rhyw*; in noun after adjective, in second part of compound noun, in title after proper name, in adjective or 'genitive' after feminine singular noun, in object after inflected verb, in complement after *bod* and *wyf*, in subject after adverbial expression, in adverbial 'accusative' of time or distance, in noun-expression after conjugated preposition, in vocative, in reduplications like *pell bell*.
7. in feminine singular noun or adjective after *y*, in adjective or noun after *yn* in complement-sense, in feminine singular after *un*, after *cyn, mor*.
8. after *saith, wyth*, except in *blynedd, blwydd, diwrnod*.
9. after *fy, yn* in local sense, in *blynedd, blwydd, diwrnod* after *un, pum, saith, wyth, naw, deng, ugain, can*.

It will be seen that 6. is far more used than 2.–5., 7.–9., second only to 1. (possibly with 5., 7., where they coincide, first in some words). (Hence the occasional re-mutations referred to in n. 22.)

Within this system a particular initial sound may be stated as a certain range of variation within an articulatory position,[23] e.g. "radical *p*" as labial stop voiceless in two rows – fricative in three – voiced stop in three – voiceless nasal in one, "radical *b*" as labial

conception of the word-form justifies the distinction in traditional grammar of the "radical" form. Further (diachronic) evidence is the re-mutation of what is originally softened form treated as new radical, e.g. of *beunyddiol* adjective from adverb *beunydd* from *peunydd*, or colloquial *hen fobol* from *bobl* from *pobl*, since this presupposes a distinctive radical slot for what is exceptionally frequent for its type to fall into.

[23] This happens to be true of Welsh, no mutation involving a distinctive change of articulatory position; it is not quite true of Irish, see below [, n. 28; also the lenition of *d, t* is heterorganic phonically, and phonologically falls together with *gh, sh/h*].

stop voiced in five – fricative in three – nasal in one, "radical *m*" as labial nasal (voiced) in six – fricative in three. Or, eliminating what is non-distinctive between the columns, labial voiceless – fricative – voiced – nasal, labial voiced ('oral stop') – fricative – nasal, nasal – fricative.

At this point we reach the level of abstraction at which the mutations are traditionally described – as four ("mutations"): "radical", "soft" (non-existent only in vowel-initial), "nasal" (only *ptcbdg*), "aspirate" (only *ptc*, vowel). These are phonologically describable as: "soft" – voiced in relation to ("radical") voiceless stop or liquid, fricative in relation to voiced stop (including nasal),[24] "nasal" – nasal in relation to oral stop; "aspirate" – fricative in relation to voiceless stop, voiceless in relation to vocalic initial.

A similar procedure for Irish[25] yields strikingly different results, e.g. what is there phonologically identifiable as *p* (i.e. with Welsh *p* as above) will, within the mutationsystem, be labial voiceless – fricative – voiced, and *t* will be apical voiceless – glottal fricative (voiceless) – apical voiced; and there are a greater number of such units, including e.g. fricative labial voiceless – zero – fricative labial voiced (*f, fh, bhf*) and fricative apical – glottal – stop (apical) (*s, sh, ts*).[26]

The phonological groupings (leaving aside the *t–* of *h–*, *–*, *n–*, *t–* [, and of *s–*, *sh–*, *ts–*]) amount to three, not four: "radical, "lenited" ("aspirated" – usually fricative (fricative in relation to stop except *n*, weak in relation to non-stop and *n*), "eclipsed" – nasal in relation to voiced stop [and to zero (vocalic initial)], voiced in relation to voiceless.

How will the methods of comparative descriptive linguistics, as

[24] Or, to cover *g/-*, non-stop in relation to voiced stop.
[25] One language from each of Brythonic and Goidelic is assumed sufficient for the present exposition; within each group the correspondence is decisively closer, a fact assumed in subsequent genetic considerations.
[26] The order is that deriving from placing functional series (a lesser number) in order to correspond to functionally comparable Welsh ones; reversing the last two phonological divisions ("lenited" ("aspirated") and "eclipsed") might give a more economical phonological description, e.g. *f*: non-stop labial voiceless – voiced – zero.

proposed by Allen,[27] apply here? Can a system be set up covering the two languages more economically than the two separate systems?

On the phonological level this is possible to the limited extent that m/f and m/mh are identifiable without complication (as nasal – fricative), as are the bdg sets (as voiced stop – fricative – nasal), also ll/l, rh/r and l/l, r/r as strong – weak.[28]

Turning to the functional series, and assuming a complex process of identification of grammatical and other functions,[29] one may identify [(still purely descriptively)] series in the two languages, and, to generalize in terms of the phonological groupings (but cf. n. 31), it seems possible to identify Irish radical with Welsh radical and aspirate, Irish aspirate with Welsh soft, Irish eclipsed with Welsh nasal.[30]

It should be noted that this identification is independent of genetic relation between the particular sounds in the particular words showing the phonological or morphonological series, e.g. it holds as much between [Welsh] *ei geffyl* and [Irish] *a cheann* (or *a thír* – or *a fhear*[31]) as between *ei geffyl* and *a chapall* or *ei ben* and *a cheann* or *ei dir* and *a thír* (just as within the language the relation does as much between *ei geffyl* and *ei ben* (or *ei wr*, but does not show in *ei ffon*) as between *ei geffyl* and *ei gi*).

But now we come to the (quite distinct) question: can the morphonological units of the one language, e.g. Welsh m or f, be identified *genetically* with morphonological units of the other, e.g. Irish m

---

[27] *Op. cit.*, especially p. 90.

[28] [to use the customary terminology for the proto-Celtic opposition; the Goidelic opposition is in fact one of articulatory positions in l, as also in n.]

[29] It would lead too far to embark here on any exposition of this highly interesting process and controversies that would attach to it (cf. Allen, especially p. 79; "General Linguistics and Comparative Philology", especially p. 168 [Appendix B, p. 105]).

[30] This on a coarse-grain mesh or statistical abstraction that allows only one to one (or two), not fractional, correspondence of phonological groupings.

[31] Thus the identification is irrespective of the kind of interdependence of levels advocated by Palmer (see n. 21). The identification is of "x plus y-modification of noun" as meaning 'his' (or of "y-modification in certain syntagmas" as implying 'feminine singular', etc., etc.), where the phonological exponents of x (*ei*, *a*) and y ("lenition") (etc.) are immaterial.

or *mh*, and what then, genetically, is the status of the morphonological alternation?[32]

Or, to put it dynamically, how are the present mutation-systems
to be traced back to before the languages were differentiated out of
the original dialect-complex?

(The present *functional series* within each language do not in
their entirety go back to its earliest records; neither do the phonological groupings. Thus somewhat different mutation-systems have
to be set up for the earliest known states of each language.)

What *can* be traced back to original Celtic are the majority of the
individual sounds involved and the generality of the functional
contexts, e.g. *d* – in both languages (and e.g. feminine singular
syntagma as a context of lenition).

All the radicals can be straightforwardly derived as part of the
general Celtic sound-correspondences (in the genetic sense of morphemic meaning-sound identification[33]), e.g. Welsh *dyn*, Irish *duine*.

The non-radicals are more involved, e.g. while radical *d* in the
one language "is" radical *d* in the other, "non-radical *d*" is Welsh
soft of *t*, Irish eclipsis of *t*. (But phonologically, this different distribution of phonological *d* (comprising radical and non-radical) is no
different from that of radicals like Irish *s*, Welsh *h*, *s*, or Irish *f*,
Welsh *gw*, (loan) *ff*.) [Cf. above at n. 18.]

Full explanation presupposes (as does much of Celtic sound-
correspondences already assumed) reconstruction of proto-Celtic
in the light of comparison with other IE branches.[34] On this basis
it becomes clear that mutation was caused, at that stage, as external
sandhi by the final sound or other feature of the preceding word.

Briefly, functional series 6. is derived (analogy apart) from
intervocalic position, e.g. after *ei*, 'his', from **esi̯o*;

9. from post-nasal position, e.g. after *yn* from **en*;

3., 4. and 5. from [certain geminations], e.g. after *ei*, 'her', from

---

[32]   This would be the point for a statement of Palmer's type excluded in n. 31.
[33]   Cf. "General Linguistics and Comparative Philology" [Appendix B] II-IV
(and n. 32 above).
[34]   [see K. Jackson, *Language and History in Early Britain* (Edinburgh, 1953).
Cf. Appendix E.]

esiās; after *a* from *aggos* (cf. the pre-vocalic form /ag/ *ac*);

2. by analogy with 3. (and see 1.);

7. as 6., but for *ll* and *rh* with phonetic "obstruction of mutation" by the Old Welsh final consonant of the word preceding, e.g. after *yn* (O.W. also *yn*) from *endo*, or feminine after *y* (O.W. *yr*);

8. as 6. for *ptc*;

1. from other positions.

Thus what in present Celtic languages is an elaborate system of phonological alternations depending in multiplex ways on grammatical (and lexical) context,[35] "was" (analogical shapings aside) once a set of sounds in different phonetic environments.

---

[35] [cf. J. Ellis, "The Grammatical Status of Initial Mutation", *Lochlann*, III (1965), pp. 315–330, and references there.]

Appendix D

RANK-BOUND TRANSLATION AND AREAL CONVERGENCE

Rank-bound translation has various applications, e.g. in theoretical linguistic exposition (cf. above, 2.21, etc.), in translation theory (above, 1.31), as part of a theoretical basis for machine translation (Halliday, "Linguistics and MT"), or in the study of "practical" translation[1] or of language-teaching.

One application within theoretical comparative linguistics, adduced above in n. 37 on p. 29, is the demonstration of a certain kind of likeness between languages, namely that exhibited by certain languages in a relation of areal convergence. (This is not to say that some components of this likeness will not also be exhibited by "typologically alike" languages in general (and deserve further investigation in connection with the possible "textual" criteria of typology mentioned in 1.212 (n. 6), 2.3, and Appendix G), or that they will not also tend (to the extent that genetic relation has remained close enough for typological correspondence to subsist, cf. above (1.224) at n. 12) to be exhibited by languages related genetically as wholes; but as will be seen from the examples below it is striking how some languages belonging to a convergence area show such likeness to each other in a greater degree than to other languages.)

The example taken here is from the Balkan convergence area.[2] Examples of varying cogency would doubtless be provided by other suggested convergence areas, possibly in the measure in which they do conform to the concept of areal convergence (on which see Ap-

---

[1] See further Ure, Rodger and Ellis, *Sonn: Sleep*, forthcoming (especially § 1).

[2] The examples are from the literary languages (in the case of Greek, δημοτική), e.g. Bulgarian feature 7 below is specifically literary, feature 4 could include Rumanian and Greek dialects; a more delicate mesh including dialects might reveal rather more of a continuum through the relevant parts of the Peninsula.

pendix F; the individual examples below of N.W. European languages help to show that N. W. European linguistic community is not areal convergence in the same close sense as Balkan is).

(Whether therefore this demonstration of likeness could be elevated into a criterion of degree of conformity to the concept would require further investigation; the (systemic) methods proposed, for wider purposes, in Appendix F would seem to demand at least equal, if complementary, consideration for this.)

In any case, the examples given have not been produced by the most rigorous[3] method of rank-bound translation described above in 2.2221 with objective probabilities for each item at each rank derived from textual examination (nor with the source-language already grammatically described in the kind of detail that English and French have been (1.31)), but rather by the analyst's intuition;[4] and they are of one very short text (John 3.14): so that the whole argument is provisional.[5]

In order to set off the interrelations of the Balkan languages against their correspondences with other languages – and to exemplify the method generally (and with some N.W. European languages) – the rank-bound translation into English is made not only from Macedonian, Bulgarian, Rumanian, Modern Greek (δημοτική) and Albanian, and from Serbo-Croat and Turkish (peripheral Balkan languages (cf. Appendix F, pp. 144, 147)), but also from Slovene, Slovak and Ukrainian (to compare with Macedonian, Bulgarian and Serbo-Croat), Latin, Italian and French (to compare with Rumanian), the Greek of the biblical original (to compare with Modern Greek), German, Danish and Scottish Gaelic, and (for greater typological diversity) Chinese.

First a Balkan language is "rank-bound translated" up to clause-

---

[3] On the degrees of rigour in rank-bound translation cf. *Somn: Sleep*, § 2.
[4] Supplemented for the Rumanian by Miss J. N. Ure; I am also indebted to Mr S. Selim for assistance with the Macedonian text. The Modern Greek text too has had to be edited (into δημοτική).
[5] A further theoretical restriction to be noted is that a language making (for a given text) fewer distinctions than (for the text here) the target-language selected here, English, would show less difference between the languages generally, one making more distinctions might show more difference between the Balkan languages themselves.

rank, then the other Balkan languages and the other languages are given rank-bound translations where they differ from the first (at points where they differ only in sequence, the first item concerned is "translated" at morpheme-rank). For the first Balkan language is selected Macedonian, as being on the whole central in Balkan interrelations (cf. Appendix F, p. 147).

The index numbers in the texts in the Balkan languages refer to the list of relevant Balkan features given after the rankbound translation from Turkish.

In order to maximize the information, there are some departures from the principle (above, 1.31) of "translating" grammatical items by "X".

Macedonian

||| И | како што | Mojcej | ja (4) | подигна (6) | змијата (5) | во пустињата (5), ||
M   and XX   XX   Moses XX X raise X   snake the X   in desert the X
W   and how what Moses her   raised   the snake   in the desert
G   and   as   Moses her   raised   the snake   in the desert
C   and just as Moses lifted up the serpent in the wilderness
така | треба (6) да (1) биде издигнат | и Синот (5) на (3) Човекот (5) |||
M   so must X   that be X   out raise X and son the X X   man   the X
W   so must   that will be raised   and the son of/to the man
G   in the same way must be raised   also the man's son
C   so also the Son of Man must be lifted up

Bulgarian

||| И | както | Мойсей | издигна (6) | змията (5) | в пустинята (5), || така |
M   how X   out raise X
W   as
трябва (6) да (1) бъде издигнат | и Синът (5) на (3) човека (5) (7) |||
M   the X X

Rumanian

||| Şi | după cum | a(2) înălţat | Moise | şarpele(5) | în pustie, ||
M   after how have X X   in high X   desert
W   after how   has   raised   desert
     tot aşa | trebuie să(1) fie înălţat | şi Fiul(5) omului (5,3) |||
M   all X so   be X in high   the X
W   whole so   is   of the man

Modern Greek

||| Καὶ | καθὼς | ὁ Μωϋσῆς | ὕψωσε | τὸν ὄφι | στὴν ἐρημία, ||

M   down as the X Moses X raise X the X snake X in the X desert X
W   as   the   the   the
      οὕτω | πρέπει νὰ(1) ὑψωθῇ | ὁ Γιὸς τοῦ ἀνθρώπου(3) |||
M   this X   raise X X   the X son X the X   X
W   the   of the of a man

Albanian

||| Edhe | sikundrë | Moisiu | ngriti | lart | gjarperinë(5) | ndë
M   as   raise X   up   X the
W   as   up
G   up
shkretëtiret (5, 3), || kështu | duhetë të (1) ngrihetë | lart |
M   X the   raise X   up
W   is raised   up
G   up
edhe i Bir'i njeriut (5, 3) |||
M   X   X   Xthe
W   X   X of the man

Serbo-Croat

||| И | као што | Мојсије | подиже | змију | у пустињи, || тако | треба | и
M   as X X   X raise X   snake X   desert X
W   as what

Син човечји | да (1) се подигне |||
M   son X man X X   himself X raise X
W   man's   himself raises

Turkish

||| Ve | Musanın | çölde | yılanı (7) | yukarı | kaldırdığı | gibi, ||
M   X desert at snake X   top   raiseX Xhislike
W   Moses' in the desert   top   his raising like
G   Moses   up   raise   as
      böylece | Insanoğlu da | yukarı | kaldırılmak gerektir (6) |||
M   this so -ly man son his also top   raise X   X necessary is
W   Son of Man   top   to be raised
G   up

Balkan (Grammatical) Features Exemplified Above

1. Conjunction with finite verb (Rumanian, Greek and Albanian Subjunctive) instead of infinitive (Macedonian and Greek no infinitive at all).   (M, B, R, G, A (SC))

2. Past tense with *have* + p. p. (in spoken standard Rumanian entirely

replaces inflected Preterite *(înălţă)*, in Macedonian (transitives) (има подигнато), Greek (ἔχει ὑψώσει), Albanian *(ka ngrit)* a Present Perfect)).   (M, R, G, A)

3. Syncretism of genitive and dative.   (M, B, R, G, A)
4. Anticipatory object pronoun (in Albanian (. . . *e ngriti* . . .), if "the object has already been referred to" (is part of *given*)). (M, A)
5. Postposed definite article.   (M, B, R, A)
6. Verbal system of renarration, etc. (the "direct" forms here would if "renarrative" (including, in Bulgarian and Turkish, "assertive")[6] be подигнал, требало, (е) издигнал, трябвало, *gerek imiş(tir)*)).   (M, B, T)
7. Nominative and accusative distinguished only in definite, Turkish, in noun-head nominal groups only in masculine singular definite, Bulgarian.   (B, T)

Slovene

```
||| In | kakor | je | Mojzes | povišal | kačo | v puščavi, ||
M       how X be X         X highXX snakeX desert X
W          as   is
        tako | mora biti povišan | Sin človekov |||
M               be X X high X sonX man  XX
W               to be           man's
```

Slovak

```
||| A | jako | Mojžiš | povýšil | hada | na púšti, || tak | musí
M      as      Mojžiš    X highXX snakeX  X desertX
W      as                              on
       být' povýšený | Syn človeka |||
M      beX X high XX  sonX man  X
W      to be              of the man
```

Ukrainian

```
||| И, | як | Мойсей | підняв | угору | гадюку | в пустині, ||
M    as        under take X X  X hill X  snake X  desert X
W    as                        up
G                              up
так | мусить бути піднятий | і Син чоловічий |||
M             be X under take X X  son X  man X X
W             to be                man's
```

---

[6] Cf. above, 1.333, pp. 28-9.

Latin

||| Et | sicut | Moyses | exaltavit | serpentem | in deserto, ||
M   so that   X out high X X snake X down connect XX
W   as
        ita | exaltari oportet | Filium hominis |||
M   out high XX   son X man X
W   to be raised   of the man

Italian

||| E | come | Mosè | innalzò | il serpente | nel deserto, ||
M   as   in highX theX snake in theX desert
W   as
        così | bisogna || che | il Figliuol | dell'uomo | sia innalzato |||
M   X care X that theX son X XtheX man beX in high
W   it is necessary that   of the   is
G   it is necessary that
C   so it is necessary that   the Son of Man should be lifted up

French

||| Et | comme | Moïse | éleva | le serpent | dans le désert, ||
M   as   raiseX theX snake   theX desert
W   as
        de même | il faut || que | le Fils de l'homme | soit élevé |||
M   of sameX XX   that theX son of theX man be X
W   of same he   that   is
G   it is necessary that
C   so it is necessary   that the Son of Man should be lifted up

Ancient Greek

||| καὶ | καθὼς | Μωυσῆς | ὕψωσε | τὸν ὄφιν | ἐν τῇ ἐρήμῳ, ||

M   down as   X raise X the X snake X   the X desert X
W   as
        οὕτως | ὑψωθῆναι δεῖ | τὸν υἱὸν τοῦ ἀνθρώπου |||
M   this X raise X X must X the X son X the X man X
W   to be raised   of the of a man

German

||| Und | wie | Moses | in der Wüste | eine Schlange | erhöhet hat, ||
M   how   in theX   a X snake   X highX haveX
W   how   has
        also | muss | des Menschen Sohn | erhöhet werden |||
M   the X man X sonX X high X become X
W   man's   son   to become

Danish

||| Og | ligesom | Moses | ophøjede | slangen | i ørkenen, ||

M   like as   up high X
W   as
       saaledes | bør | Menneskesønnen | ophøjes |||
M   so X   must X   man   X son theX up high himself
W   the Son of Man   to be raised
G   the Son of Man

Scottish Gaelic

||| Agus | mar | a thog | Maois | suas | an nathair | 's an fhàsach, ||
M   as   X raiseX   up   theX snake   theX desert
W   as   X   up
G   up
       is ann | mar sin | is èigin | do Mhac an duine | bhi air a thogail
M   beX in him as that beX necessity to son theX man beX on his raiseX
W   is there   as that is necessity   to son the man to be on this to raise
G   to the man's son
       suas |||
M   up
W   up

Chinese[7]

||| Móxī | zài kuàngyě | zěnyàng | jǔ | shé, || rén zǐ | yě |
M   rub west at waste wild X kind raise snake man son also
W   Moses at desert   how   raise snake man son also
       bì | zhào yàng | bèi jǔ | qylái |||
M   must reflect kind   X raise rise come
W   must reflect kind   X raise   rise
G   according to the pattern

---

[7] For the transcription see above, n. 66 on p. 55.

Appendix E

ON LINGUISTIC PREHISTORY

In "The Nature and Use of Proto-Languages" (*Lingua*, X, 1961, pp. 18–37) Ernst Pulgram urges among other, incontestable, arguments against the extreme (pro-"realism") position of R. A. Hall (pp. 22–23), that the supposed reality of any reconstructed "language" is dependent upon its remaining the earliest stage reconstructed for the given observed languages. "For as soon as we have relegated Reconstructed Proto-Indo-European to any place other than the ultimately accessible apex of the pyramid of family reconstruction, have placed it in any but the terminal position, as some day perhaps we shall have to do, we shall have put it on a spot where, apart from its congenital lack of authenticity in form and substance, the very existence of a Real Proto-Indo-European in the customary sense of the word is no longer implied" (pp. 34–35).

His rejection of Hall and others' views is wholly justified, and no reinforcement of it is needed here.[1]

But the further argument seems to me to be throwing the baby (of comparative philological substance) out with the bathwater (of comparative philologists' dogmatism); and specifically, while it is correct to imply that the hypotheses of comparative philology must be subject to constant revision,[2] Pulgram's conception of the role, "nature and use", and content of reconstruction would allow of no core of continuous identity in our successive hypotheses, as far as the demarcation and content of proto-languages are concerned, no point in any such hypothesis since the next will (not merely

---

[1] See "Some Problems in Comparative Linguistics", p. 57, n. 1 (Appendix C, p. 118) (cf. "General Linguistics and Comparative Philology", p. 169 (Appendix B, p. 107)).

[2] Cf. *GLCP*, p. 142 (Appendix B, p. 80).

may) overthrow it lock, stock and barrel. This methodologically
nihilistic implication in itself does not invalidate his conclusion;
but if valid the conclusion, with the implication, would render
nugatory any but the sketchiest of comparative philological work,
the very development and filling in of which he assumes and seeks
to further. Fortunately there seem to me sufficient grounds for
rejecting the conclusion.

Essentially Pulgram's argument on this subject may be outlined
as follows. If, for example, we knew nothing about the historical
conditions of the introduction of Latin into the Iberian peninsula,
or as little as we do about the stage in the prehistory of the IE
languages usually represented as the IE proto-language, we should
assert the existence of a proto-Ibero-Romance.[3] In fact, since we
can trace the Romance languages of the peninsula back to Latin[4]
dialects, and in principle to Latin, and these back to community
with other IE languages, we know that proto-Ibero-Romance may

[3]   It would perhaps be unfair to Pulgram to press for clarification in Izzo's
remarks which he appends to support his case, of "the existence of Proto-Hispa-
no-Portuguese seems somewhat more plausible than the existence of Proto-
Hispano-Roumanian" (for it is hard to believe anyone would argue that *only*
"extra-linguistic information" would be our ground for making a more radical
separation between East and West Romance than within West Romance – for
chronological implications of "radicalness" of separation see below); but as
suggested below there appear to be similar unevennesses in his own exposition.
[4]   As to the argument (p. 21) that "a linguist ignorant of the significant non-
linguistic circumstances" could view Latin and Italian as sister languages and
"rightly feel entitled to reconstruct from them a proto-language . . . that such a
one never existed will not show in its physiognomy", see J. Holt, *Proceedings of
the VIIth International Congress of Linguists (1952)* (London, 1956), p. 98, on
relational asymmetry between successive etats de langue (in his terms Latin and
Italian would be a case of "all the elements of one system [determining] all
elements of another, such systems [being] two stages of the same language",
(while "they belong to different languages if the direction of determination is
shifting from one [element] to another") with Latin as "the system with constants", therefore "the older one", Italian "the stage with the variables", therefore "the younger one"); it is indeed not the physiognomy in itself that shows
whether a linguistic construct had any existence (otherwise any artificial language
informed by knowledge of typological feasibilities would lay claim to "reality" (as
a "natural" language!)) but the relation of this to the physiognomies of the observed related languages (and not merely typologically to any and all observed
languages!), in this case the actual identifiability of it with relevant parts of Latin
itself.

be a complete fiction. (Cf. p. 34, "Proto-Ibero-Romanic turned out to be Latin."[5]) Similarly if we could trace the IE languages back to community with the Semitic languages (Pulgram: "Proto-IE-Semitic"), or even since some already trace them back to community with Hittite other than as proto-IE (Pulgram: "Proto-Indo-Hittite"),[6] we should, or even do, reject "proto-IE".

The assumptions about the nature of the existence of languages through time underlying this argument are not entirely clear, and I may have misapprehended them, though if so the argument seems directed (apart from the already otherwise vulnerable positions referred to above of Hall and c.) against Aunt Sallies. But if I have understood aright Pulgram assumes that the speech of a (linguistic) community is (or at the least may be) *either* a "language", one and indivisible, *or* a conglomeration of dialects not essentially distinct from the speech of other communities. (Stated thus the assumption would seem palpably absurd, and yet not only does his argument appear otherwise not to cohere, but in fact other linguists[7] too have been known to deny the contrary, by questioning (scil. even as a relative concept in the sense of being conditional on discrete idiolectal and institutional (-linguistic) (etc.) facts generalized from) the continuous and distinctive identity of languages.[8])

All speech is indeed made up of dialectal, ultimately idiolectal

[5] To anticipate summarily our subsequent argument (and observation of difficulties in citing a cohesive position from Pulgram), here, in the bald equation ("Proto-Indo-European may turn out to be language X of the larger tree just as Proto-Ibero-Romanic turned out to be Latin"), may be said to be manifested the essence of the *non sequitur*, for if the equation is to be valid proto-IE would have to turn out to be not language X of the larger tree but the apex of the tree itself.

[6] That such a tracing is now generally discredited (on some of the issues and references involved cf. *GLCP*, p. 155, n. 89 (Appendix B, p. 92, n. 88) as well as Pulgram, p. 35, with n. 18) is immaterial to Pulgram's argument.

[7] E.g. those criticized in *GLCP* (Appendix B).

[8] Presenting themselves in controversy as crucial only when the issue within general linguistics concerns genetic linguistics (see *GLCP*, pp. 147–151 (Appendix B, pp. 84–9), and *SPCL*, p. 57 (especially n. 16) (Appendix C, p. 117)), such questions pose the indispensability to a complete linguistics (or, according to one's terminology, complex of linguistic sciences) of an institutional linguistics based on observed dialectological and other relevant facts (vide T. Hill, "Institutional Linguistics", *Orbis*, VII, 1958, pp. 441–455 (especially 454–5)).

(and within idiolect ontogenetic), variations, variations in any one linguistic feature overlapping those in any other (except over really decisive geographical discontinuities[9] such as (scil. still for any *one* "feature") in modern conditions of communication have probably ceased to exist for the vast majority of mankind (if for example any one "international" neologism (complete borrowing or calque) counts as a feature)); but, and this is the important point for linguistics as a generalizing science, any one feature is a tiny proportion of any language, dialect or idiolect ("tongue"), and as regards *the bulk of* features within any tongue, variations follow a pattern of overlap as between "dialects" (demarcated relatively by bundles of isoglosses) but of discontinuity as between the "languages" that the dialects make up. ("Language" here not in an institutional sense, e.g. German-Dutch is here one "language".) Finally, over the years and through generations these patterns shift and new discontinuities appear, nodal points in the dialectic of social (geographical etc.) community and linguistic intercomprehensibility on the basis of which the bulk of features pursue their common development. (See *SPCL*, pp. 55–56, 57 (and n. 16) (Appendix C, pp. 115–6, 117), *GLCP* pp. 147–50 (Appendix B, pp. 84–87).)

So, for example, it has been generally accepted that there was a period during which what "are" now the distinct Germanic "languages" (English, "German-Dutch", Frisian, continental Scandinavian, Icelandic-Faroese (as a minimum)), "were" one dialect continuum, distinct from other IE dialect continua (e.g. Celtic, Italic, Slavonic). Now according to Pulgram this was not so, precisely because it can be accepted that (to use our terms) there was an earlier period during which all the IE "dialect continua" were *one* dialect continuum, and there is no knowing how to split up this continuum into groupings of the observed distinct languages like English, French, Russian, etc.[10]

---

[9] For a general discussion of discontinuities between "tongues" (needing more particularization in some directions) see Hill, p. 443.

[10] Cf. Pulgram, p. 25, on what prevents the linguist "from comparing, for example, English and Russian (except on the level of Proto-Germanic and Proto-Slavic)" – the use of the vague term "compare" (proper, thus unqualified, to general comparative linguistics) here for one or more specific operations in

Indeed, this last argument of Pulgram's would have some application if we had only fragments of the evidence for IE that we actually possess – but then the previous arguments would lose their basis in sufficient IE data! As it is, Pulgram has not demonstrated, by mere extrapolation from Romance philology (cf. pp. 20–21, n. 2), that the evidence traditionally adduced for Proto-Germanic etc. (understood relatively as "discontinuities" at given times (approximately defined)) is not cogent; and no amount of insistence that comparative philology has not (yet[11]) (relevant) quantitative methods (pp. 25–28, cf. p. 29 *init.*) will in fact conjure away this evidence (however much the evidence may stand in need of further codification and systematization).[12]

It remains to emphasize (as I have done in more detail elsewhere[13]) the "relative", probabilistic and statistically (if as yet unformalized (n. 7)) founded nature of genetic relation, not only as regards the identity, nature and extent of items reconstructed (Pulgram, pp. 20–21 n.), which are at best asymptotic to the systems of a "real

---

genetic comparative linguistics, with all their differentiated results, surely helps to create the confusion that characterizes his thesis.

[11]   To Pulgram's references (p. 25, n. 8) on quantification of genetic comparative method, especially IE, add A. S. C. Ross, "Philological Probability Problems", *Journal of the Royal Statistical Society*, Series B (*Methodological*), Vol. XII, No. 1 (1950), pp. 19–59, and references there. (Ross's treatment of the genetic problem, pp. 19–30, is open to two criticisms: a. all that his evidence proves is common origin of *items* (cf. *GLCP*, p. 152 (Appendix B, p. 89)) (not only because as Pulgram pp. 25–26 says lexical evidence is insufficient but because the lexical evidence is not organized and for example "common ideas like names of relatives" (p. 20) in any way circumscribed or otherwise evaluated (beyond there being 1,000 of them) (see *GLCP*, pp. 148–9 (Appendix B, pp. 85–86)); b. the data are unnecessarily (and as regards disembodied "ideas" unverifiably?) restricted by taking "the word in each language for . . ." instead of words of potentially related meaning that can be related by phonological correspondence (cf. *GLCP*, pp. 144–5 (Appendix B, pp. 81–82)) (a criterion for relevant potentiality of relation of meaning is admittedly something not yet made rigorous, but such restriction is already certainly no more arbitrary than the "ideas" at present figuring in Ross's method) – cf. p. 44, Sir W. Elderton in discussion, on *dog-Hund-hound.*)

[12]   *GLCP*, pp. 170–1, 145–6 (Appendix B, pp. 108–9, 82–83), *SPCL*, p. 58 (Appendix C, p. 120).

[13]   *GLCP*, pp. 160 ff. (Appendix B, pp. 97 ff.), *SPCL*, p. 57, n. 19 (Appendix C, p. 119).

language" and at some levels cannot resemble one at all,[14] but also as regards the "sections of genetic history" (*GLCP*, pp. 154–155 (Appendix B, pp. 91–3)) to which they can be attributed, with or without enough precision[15] of these to speak of "languages", dialect continua with discontinuity.

But this in no way gives grounds (where no specific revolutionary evidence is forthcoming on some particular point) for failing to see each hypothesis as a stepping stone to the next in the sense that (by and large, allowing for any "revolutionary evidence") its main substance is incorporated in it. The healthy scepticism from which Pulgram starts should not be allowed to blind us to the secure results already long achieved and progressively built upon.

To exemplify "sections of genetic history" and their crucial role in any elaboration in detail of genetic comparative linguistics, let us take an example that has been well treated (with a wealth of detail from historical records, for Brythonic by Kenneth Jackson),[16] that of the development of the consonants in the Celtic languages.

Here we are faced with the fact that the contemporary languages, which are now indubitably "discontinuous" (Goidelic from Brythonic and Irish from Scottish Gaelic, Welsh from Breton), have features of development in common (e.g. the lenition of voiced stops), and others divergent (e.g. the lenition, and the nasalization/eclipsis, of voiceless stops; the Brythonic spirant mutation; within Goidelic the differing "eclipsis" of Irish and Scottish Gaelic (dialects)), as well as others at first sight of controversial interpretation (e.g. the mutation of the liquids).

The historical explanation entails a distinguishing of a common (Insular) Celtic "genetic section", common Goidelic and Brythonic ones, and further communities of development such as Jackson

[14]   *GLCP*, p. 169 (Appendix B, p. 107).

[15]   As probably (on present agreed evidence) there is not enough precision to speak of "proto-Italo-Celtic" (to take one example (another is proto-West-Germanic) that Pulgram lumps together with e.g. proto-Germanic). Cf. *GLCP*, p. 155, nn. 88–90 (Appendix B, pp. 92–3, n. 87–89).

[16]   K. Jackson, *Language and History in Early Britain* (Edinburgh, 1953); on the general problem of the initial mutations see also Appendix D and the references in J. Ellis, "The Grammatical Status of Initial Mutation", *Lochlann*, III (196)5, pp. 315–330.

traces for Welsh-Cornish-Breton (pp. 18–30, where he demonstrates that language-separation does not "make a neat and tidy picture" (p. 18), but none the less ultimately takes effect – precisely our notion of approximately defined sections).

To the first belongs the differing length ("gemination") of consonants in different phonetic conditions, to the second (cf. Jackson p. 23) the development of the geminates (in Brythonic semi-geminates; Jackson, p. 546), into the "non-lenited", "radical", consonants, and of the non-geminates into the lenited consonants (in Breton still of differing duration; Jackson, p. 474) (and in Brythonic of the initial full geminates into fricatives), to the third such specific developments as Scottish Gaelic analogical renasalization of the eclipsis of *ptc* (e.g. *nan t-* ~ Irish *na dt-*) and nasal sandhi after proclitic -*n*, e.g. *an cù* (Lewis ə ŋuː). (*Sandhi*, because it is one of the differences between this and Welsh nasal *mutation* (that invalidate any talk of convergent development) that its contexts of occurrence can be defined phonologically (whereas the Welsh phenomenon occurs after one proclitic with vowel-final (in all non-nasal occurrences) in Literary Welsh, as well as *yn* "in" and a few other isolated occurrences).)

Jackson p. 547 refers to "the time when e.g. *t* became a full *d* in British and a full *th* in Irish, and these were felt as phonemes distinct from non-lenited *tt*, *t(t)*-" (cf. 477–8 on liquid allophones[17]). In fact, the distinction becomes phonemic (whatever the phonic substance of the distinguenda), mutation no longer sandhi, when the original phonetic environment disappears, and this crucial stage belongs to the separate Goidelic and Brythonic "sections".

The distinguishing of sections inferred from the more obvious phenomena (as well as from all the other features of development besides the phonology of consonants) can then be built upon in explaining the more obscure ones, e.g. Jackson's account of the liquids (pp. 471–80).

To the Celticist all this (aside from loose ends still debated) is indisputable; we refer to it here, in summary, because, like innumerable other concrete findings, it would be undermined if it were

[17]   "*fully* fledged *perceptible* phonemic λ, ρ̣" (my italics).

true that one proto-language, e.g. proto-Celtic (or proto-IE) cancels out another, e.g. proto-Brythonic (or proto-Celtic).

In concluding it may help to clarify the issue to sum up the two models of hypothesis-generation contrasted here (and to be evaluated in application to comparative philological material): Pulgram's one of abrupt reversal of hypotheses, with unitary proto-languages at each successive "terminal" stage; ours of a general direction of refinement of hypotheses, with progressively defined "sections of genetic history", and a "proto-language" (discontinuity of one dialect continuum from others) once set up, in general kept.

POSSIBLE COMPARISONS OF BALKAN AND
NORTH-WEST EUROPEAN LINGUISTIC COMMUNITY, WITH
REFERENCE TO SYSTEM-REDUCTION METHOD OF
QUANTIFICATION

1. *Areal Linguistic Community ("Convergence areas")*

The purpose of this paper is to outline one possible approach to some of the problems of "Balkan linguistics" by setting against them certain possible parallels and differences in another region and considering the possible extent of application to such confrontations of methods of descriptive linguistic comparison and its quantification.

The choice of the geographically opposite "quarter" of Europe is of course partly determined by the writer's own provenance and other linguistic interests. But, as may be gathered from § 2, this linguistic area or set of areas does provide certain combinations of phenomena which might be found in few other regions.[1]

There is no one recognised term in English for языковый союз or *Sprachbund*.[2] Terms in use include *linguistic area* (H. V. Velten's (1943) translation of *Sprachbund*),[3] *area-grouping*,[4] (*areal*) *group*,[5] *affinité linguistique*,[6] or *affinity*,[7] (*features of*) *linguistic unity*,[8] etc.

Perhaps the likeliest candidate for acceptance now is Weinreich's

---

[1] Cf. A. Martinet, *Proceedings of Seventh International Congress of Linguists*, p. 123 and E. Lewy, *ibid.*, p. 128 ("Western Europe").

[2] For some history of the notion, especially in English-speaking writers, see M. B. Emeneau, "India as a linguistic area", *Language*, 32 (1956), pp. 3–16 (pp. 3–5), and references there.

[3] See Emeneau, p. 16, n. 28, and references there.

[4] C. F. Voegelin, "Influence of Area in American Indian Linguistics", *Word*, 1 (1948), pp. 54–58 (p. 58).

[5] e.g. J. H. Greenberg, *Essays in Linguistics* (Chicago, 1957), p. 67.

[6] e.g. *affinité grammaticale*, *Seventh Congress*, pp. 121 ff.

[7] U. Weinreich, "On the Compatibility of Genetic Relationship and Convergent Development", *Word*, 14 (1958), pp. 374–9 (p. 379), a property rather than a class.

[8] Ellis, *Seventh Congress*, p. 125.

convergence area,[9] though for the general phenomenon[10] represented by such areas, which moreover may break down into overlapping sub-areas,[11] it is desirable to add[12] the "transform" *areal convergence* or alternative phrasing *areal linguistic community.*

The term *areal linguistics* itself would be ambiguous, since it is more usually used[13] for "linguistic geography" or dialectological principles, e.g. in application to the history of related languages (e.g. *Seventh Congress,* pp. 149–58).

The term *linguistic community* has the disadvantage of possible confusion with the term for the particular society or community (cf. n. 7) speaking a given language (or dialect): here the term *language-communities* will be used for such societies.[14]

Different terms place an emphasis on different aspects of the phenomenon: "affinité" on resemblance (understood by Regamey, *Seventh Congress,* p. 129, as more general than Sprachbund) with or without genetic relation of some kind, "союз" or "Bund" on the involvement of discrete languages with each other in some way (cf. Weinreich, p. 379, and n. 11 above), "areal convergence" or "convergence areas" on a historical origination (convergence[15]) but at the same time, and this is a highly important aspect distinguishing the phenomenon from genetically related language-families on the one side and general typological comparison on the other,[16] on the geographical contiguity.

It is now generally agreed (if we may except Martinet, *Seventh*

---

[9] "Compatibility", p. 379 ("if necessary"), "perhaps more specifically meaningful than" Emeneau's *linguistic area.*

[10] Weinreich: convergent development; cf. n. 7.

[11] *Seventh Congress,* p. 125; Weinreich, pp. 378–9 ("ad hoc").

[12] Cf. Emeneau, p. 16, n. 28, adjective impossible with *linguistic area,* and "reverse phrase" (see n. 13).

[13] Emeneau, p. 16, n. 28: "preempted by Italian neolinguistic school".

[14] On the qualitative difference between *language-communities* and any other kind of "linguistic community" (once there is not mutual comprehension) cf. Ellis, "Some Problems in Comparative Linguistics", *Proceedings of the University of Durham Philosophical Society,* Volume I, Series B (*Arts*), No. 7 (1961), pp. 54–62 (p. 57 [Appendix C, p. 60], n. 16 (and for the limiting case of bridge-pidgins cf. 2, n. 27).

[15] Cf. n. 10 above and Martinet, *Seventh Congress,* p. 122.

[16] Cf. Greenberg, p. 67; Martinet, pp. 121–2.

Congress, pp. 122 and 123) that the process of causation is one of influence (through some form of bilingual activity[17]) of one language upon another in some particular, rather than of some direct effect of common geographical, social, etc., conditions.

Thus an alternative formulation, though one too unwieldy for a short appellation, but making clear the way in which the geographical contiguity takes effect, would be "genetic relation of parts of languages not, or not relevantly, related as languages", specifying that the "parts" in question are something more than mere small-scale lexical loans,[18] and it is upon such a conception that the following remarks are based.

2. *Balkan and North-West European Linguistic Community*

Balkan linguistic community is an accepted fact, though its exact demarcation and interpretation may be another matter. Linguistic community in North-Western Europe, distinct from wider linguistic areas (such as that of Whorf's "Standard Average European"), as specifically Balkan features are from more general ones, is by no means equally undisputed. In fact, there are undoubtedly certain major differences between the two regions which impose severe limitations upon analogy between their linguistic development and états. On the other hand, taking linguistic community in the widest sense a prima facie case may be admitted for predicating it of at least parts of this region, and proceeding to seek stricter definition of its incidence here.

The Balkan languages, it is clear enough, comprise the South Slavonic languages (with the exception of Slovene), Rumanian, Greek, Albanian, and Turkish. (Disregarding at this stage narrower geographical and chronologically conditioned distinctions.)

The "languages of North-Western Europe" would require more

---

[17] Cf. Weinreich, *Languages in Contact* (New York, 1953), passim, and K. Sandfeld, *Linguistique balkanique* (Paris, 1930), p. 214; E. Seidel, *Elemente sintactice slave în limba romînă* (Bucharest, 1958), p. 70, n. 1.

[18] Cf. Weinreich, *Contact*, p. 1, pp. 64–5, "Compatibility", pp. 378-9 ("structural isoglosses"), Ellis, "General Linguistics and Comparative Philology", *Lingua*, VII (1958), 134–174 (pp. 146–8) [Appendix B, pp. 83–4].

qualified determination, partly for reasons of the differences outlined below. If however we divide Northern Europe from Southern
(and "Central") by a line running somewhere through France and
Germany, and Western from Eastern by one of irregular shape from
the borders of (Norway-) Sweden and Finland to those of Italy and
Yugoslavia, then languages included are: the Scandinavian languages (North Germanic), the surviving Celtic languages, English,
the other West Germanic dialects other than South German, and
(Northern dialects of) French.

Among these (including the literary, national and other "stan-
dardized languages" based on the dialects) there is historical and
linguistic evidence for contacts classifiable by the categories of
institutional linguistics,[19] of various kinds at various times, e.g.:

1. Contemporary and recent modern influences in all (or most)
directions (including for example the contemporary phase of that
of both British and American English).

2. Influence of French in the modern period.

3. Various periods of Latin influence.

4. German (*Hochsprache* and Low German) influence on continental Scandinavian.

5. English influence on Celtic languages, and French on Breton.[20]

6. French influence on English, and especially on Scots.

7. French influence on Dutch-Flemish.

8. Scandinavian influence on English.

9. North-Eastern French and North-West continental West
Germanic dialect convergences.[21]

10. Celtic (Goidelic) and ("insular") Scandinavian convergen-ces.[22]

11. Germanic (Franconian) influence on French.[23]

[19]   See T. Hill, "Institutional Linguistics", *Orbis*, VII (1958), pp. 441–455.
[20]   e.g. the development of apical fricatives; or E. Hamp, "Morphological
Correspondences in Cornish and Breton", *Journal of Celtic Studies*. II (1953),
pp. 5–24 (p. 20, n. 13).
[21]   Martinet, *op. cit.*, p. 124.
[22]   *Proceedings of First International Congress of Celticists*, pp. 3–11, 73–77;
Lewy, *op. cit.*, p. 129; P. L. Henry, "The Icelandic Prepositional System", *Zeitschrift für vergleichende Sprachforschung*, 79 (1959), pp. 89–135 (esp. pp. 89,
101–5).
[23]   Bloomfield, *Language*, pp. 466–7.

12. Celtic and English convergences.[24]

13. Celtic influence on proto-French.[25]

14. Resemblances between Celtic languages and other languages of Western Europe (and North Africa) generally,[26] ascribed by some to "Iberian" or Hamitic substratum.

(The last three are in order of increasing hypotheticalness and ultimate unverifiability.)

Of these, 5, 8, 9, 10, 11, 12, 13 and (presumably) 14 qualify for the kind of conditions of contact of *vernaculars*[27] envisaged for "affinité grammaticale" by Martinet, *Seventh Congress*, pp. 121 ff., though it is to be noted that unanimity that Balkan community is predominantly of such origin[27] is not complete.

On the other hand, only 8, 11, 14 and possibly 13 and just possibly 3,[28] involve any really large-scale incidence of the kind of not merely lexical "convergences" that mark out Balkan linguistic community.

Any further formal linguistic classification (of either region), and relating of it to institutional linguistic differentia, may (for the purposes of the present argument) be left to await the carrying out of detailed application of the kind of formulation of the linguistic data to be discussed below.

The major differences distinguishing North-Western Europe

---

[24] Lewy, p. 128; and e.g. H. Wagner, *Das Verbum in den Sprachen der britischen Inseln* (Tübingen, 1959).

[25] Bloomfield, p. 469.

[26] cf. Lewy's (p. 128) English-NorthGermanic-WestRomance-Basque (and, implicitly, Celtic), and Wagner, *op. cit.*

[27] Cf. Bloomfield's distinction between "cultural and intimate borrowing", *Language*, Chapters 25 and 26, which briefly mentions areal convergence without giving it a name (p. 470), and at greater length (pp. 472–5) the allied case (treated by Weinreich, "Compatibility", p. 379, as yielding cases of areal convergence itself) where the result of convergence (between languages in a particular kind of ("upper/dominant-lower" (Bloomfield, pp. 461 ff.)) institutional relation) is a co-existing third language (in which alone the relevant speakers of each original language are "bilingual"), a pidgin or (Bloomfield) "jargon" (genetically one of the original languages (the upper (Bloomfield, p. 472)) drastically "restructured" (Ellis, "General ...", p. 150 with nn. 63–66 [Appendix B, p. 87, nn. 62–65] and references there) as in normal convergence both may be without ceasing to be two). (Weinreich, *loc. cit.*, sees e.g. the pidgins/creoles of the Caribbean as a *Sprachbund* of the upper languages.)

[28] Bloomfield, *Language*, p. 471.

from the Balkans as regards institutional linguistic conditions are the following:

1. The kind of sub-groupings of community into which the Balkan languages fall are in the case of North-Western Europe more numerous, more intricate, more differentiated chronologically, and to some extent (the exact extent is precisely the topic for closer investigation), less cohesive one with another.

2. The more recent economic, political and social history of most of the North-West European language-communities (more obvious exceptions include Scottish Gaelic, Breton, Faroese) includes a longer period of national independence and unification, etc., with its effects both internally in increasing standardization of the vernacular, the pattern of styles and registers,[29] etc., and externally in the character of interlanguage influences.

3. Following on from 2., while no Balkan language (leaving aside the special case of Turkish (itself included only in chronological divisions of community subsequent to the principal ones) and also the special relation of Medieval and Modern Greek with Classical (period prior to principal community)) has currency outside the Balkans, North-West European languages include English, French and German, all in some sense "world-languages".

A more particular point, but one possibly of some more than methodological significance (it is inter alia a symptom of 1.):

4. The Balkan land-mass with its language-communities is capable of being regarded, intuitively (and subject to the kind of objective scrutiny to be discussed later), as having a linguistic centre, a most "typically Balkan" form, or focus of relevant isoglosses, in Slavonic Macedonia. The geographical centre of North-Western Europe would be somewhere in the North Sea, and no one obvious candidate for "linguistic centre" presents itself. (Possible candidates like Scottish Gaelic and some form of English, besides offering institutionally contrasts at two extremes with (contemporary) Macedonia, fail to represent the meeting ground of all principal subgroupings, though (British) English (and perhaps

[29] See Hill, *op. cit.*, and Ellis, "Some Recent Work on German Grammar", *Archivum Linguisticum*, XIII (1962), pp. 33–49 (p. 41, n. 4).

more particularly the educated colloquial English[30] of Scotland) comes nearest to this.)

3. System-reduction Method of Quantification of Descriptive Linguistic Comparison and its Applicability to Areal Convergences

In comparative *descriptive* linguistics, comparison (the establishment of correspondence) is of systems.[31] In *genetic* comparative linguistics, i.e. the comparative linguistics of *related languages* (or languages whose relation is in question), comparison (the establishment of relation) is of items, systems having in various senses a secondary role.[32]

Comparison of languages belonging to convergence areas, as such clearly occupies an intermediate position, since here we have genetically *related items* (or items whose genetic relation is in question) in languages otherwise no different from any two or more languages being compared descriptively.[33]

More specifically, the kind of correspondences which are relevant to areal convergence are more comprehensive than those which are most directly relevant to genetic relation *of languages*[34] (though the exact degree of relevance of others is an open question[35]) and may include correspondences of system as such. E.g., Turkish-Bulgarian community in respect of the verb lies as much[36] in the systemic

---

[30] See T. Hill, *op. cit.*, pp. 450–1.

[31] See e.g. W. S. Allen, "Relationship in Comparative Linguistics", *Transactions of the Philological Society*, 1953, pp. 52–108 (p. 92) (noting that he uses "relation" for correspondence, not genetically). (System – *as opposed to item* – comparison of course entails, in the measure that linear comparison enters, *structural* comparison of corresponding texts, cf. Ellis, "On Comparative Descriptive Linguistics", *Езиковедски изследвания в чест на академик С. Младенов (Studia in honorem ... S. Mladenov)* (Sofia, 1957), pp. 555–565 [Appendix G]).

[32] See Ellis, "General ...", p. 151 with n. 75, pp. 159–60 [Appendix B, p. 88, pp. 95–97], "Some Problems", p. 58 [Appendix C, p. 120].

[33] On the qualitative distinction between set of items and language see "General ..." pp. 148–51, and cf. § 1, n. 14.

[34] See "General ...", pp. 143–8 [Appendix B, pp. 80–85].

[35] See "General ...", pp. 171–3 [Appendix B, pp. 108–10].

[36] Once given that there *is* community in the sense of genetic relation of items – degrees of conclusiveness of evidence for this are another matter, cf. "General...", (as in n. 35), *Seventh Congress*, p. 125. It may also, as in the case discussed by

oppositions "direct" (пряко изказано)/"renarrative" (преизка-
зано)/"assertive", etc., as in the distribution of participial and
auxiliary forms in their exponence (-miş(tir), -л (е)).[37]

It may therefore be of interest to examine descriptive (systemic)
comparisons within (and as between) convergence areas, in comparison[38] with those of other languages, including where applicable,
of ones in genetic relation as languages. E.g., of systems in, on the
one hand, sets (of pairs) of Balkan languages, on the other any one
Balkan language and some other language or languages, including
the Slavonic ones with each other and with non-Balkan Slavonic
languages. Or, on the one hand, say English and Celtic languages,
on the other English and other Germanic languages, etc. Or, finally, the pattern of correspondences (cf. n. 38) of the first (Balkan-
based) with the second (North-West-European-based).

This is in any case feasible as a "pattern of correspondence" to the
extent that the data of comparison, systemic correspondences, are
quantifiable. This quantifiability would be the advantage of utilizing systemic comparison.[39] Its shortcoming as a possible measure
of areal convergence is that such correspondences by no means
exhaust the relevant ones (nor in themselves are necessarily the
most relevant as *evidence* (cf. n. 36)): and this limitation must be
borne in mind, though it is no reason for not exploring the section
of data that *are* amenable to the method.

The quantification of systemic correspondence has been introduced by W. S. Allen,[40] and the method proposed here will be

---

Seidel, *op. cit.*, pp. 41–3, lie in systemic opposition without exact exponential
parallelism.

[37] See *Seventh Congress*, p. 125.

[38] Thus introducing comparison of comparisons ("metacomparison") methodologically unavoidable in order to put the basic pair-comparisons in the necessary perspective.

[39] For the present inconclusive state of quantifiability of *non-systemic* correspondence, in language-genetic relation (or even in comparison without necessarily genetic purposes, e.g. Grimes and Agard, "Linguistic Divergence in
Romance", *Language*, 35, 1959, pp. 598–604), cf. the references in A. Ellegard,
"Statistical measurement of linguistic relationship", *Language*, 35 (1959), pp.
131–156 (p. 131. nn. 1–5); cf. also Weinreich, *Contact*, p. 67.

[40] W. S. Allen, "Relationship in Comparative Linguistics", *Transactions of the
Philological Society*, 1953, pp. 52–108 (pp. 90, 92–3).

essentially his, with a minor modification originated by R. M. W. Dixon in the mathematical formulation (see n. 52). The mathematical operations rest upon a systemic statement involving any reduction possible in the number of terms from the total for the given comparable systems in the given pair of languages, so that the method as a whole may be referred to as "system-reduction".

First comparability of systems and identity of terms between languages must be established. Such comparability of any linguistic feature has been assumed here, in saying (§§ 1–3, passim) that a phenomenon in one language "is" ("comes from") one in another, or "corresponds to" it, or "resembles" it.[41] In fact, theoretically, this[42] implies some tertium quid comparationis,[43] which at the phonological and formal levels[44] may be formal meaning,[45] or at the phonological level phonic substance,[46] or at the formal level contextual meaning,[47] and this last is the basis of the correspondences here mainly referred to.[48] In what follows, the assumption will be continued that this step, in all its methodological complexity (cf. n. 48), has been taken, so that one can proceed to quantitative statement of correspondence.

It does however remain to add to Allen's schema of descriptive

[41] Genetic identity (of items themselves not necessarily descriptively identifiable) and descriptive identity (of terms in systems) are of course quite distinct (cf. references in n. 32), a distinction blurred e.g. in Ellegård, op. cit. (n. 39), p. 155.
[42] i.e. (in the first instance) the "descriptive identification" of n. 41.
[43] Cf. "On Comparative . . .", p. 556, n. 3 [Appendix G, p. 155, n. 7].
[44] M. A. K. Halliday, "Categories of the Theory of Grammar", Word, 17 (1961), pp. 241–292 (pp. 243–4).
[45] Halliday, op. cit., pp. 244–5.
[46] Allen, op. cit., pp. 95–6.
[47] Generalized from instantial and observable situations, or ones ultimately referable to observables (cf. M. A. K. Halliday, "Some Aspects of Systematic Description and Comparison in Grammatical Analysis", Studies in Linguistic Analysis, London, 1957, 55, pp. 54–67, pp. 64–5); see J. Ellis, "On Contextual Meaning", to appear in the Fifth Memorial Volume, and the references in Ellis, "Some Recent Work on German Grammar", Archivum Linguisticum, XIII, pp. 33–49 (p. 37).
[48] On the whole question, and controversies within it, see "General . . .", pp. 167–8 [Appendix B, pp. 104–5], and cf. "On Comparative", pp. 556, 563–4, 565 [Appendix G, pp. 155, 167–8, 169], and "Some Problems", p. 60, ped. [Appendix C, p. 124], and n. 30.

comparison various scales of delicacy[49] of comparison on which the schema can be made more precise.

For example, increasing restrictions may be placed on the formal complementation, of the terms in question, in co-text[50] or on contextual complementation, of the whole formal complex, in situations. E.g., we may distinguish the English tense system used in free clauses and some types of bound clauses from that used in bound clauses like "if I went".

Again, within systems, differing extent of terms or subsystems may be taken into account in the comparison. E.g. comparing English and French tense, we have least delicately on this scale English present/past/future, more delicately, with addition of English "present in" (be & -ing), "past in" (have & P. P.), "future in" (be going to), and French aller forms (more delicately still venir de).

Similarly account may be taken of uses (again possibly situationally or co-textually conditioned) in grammatically more restricted classes of lexical items classed together as exponents of the unit showing the grammatical oppositions in question. E.g., least delicately on this scale, to Scottish Gaelic tha a(g) corresponds Standard English be & -ing, but a more delicate treatment would include the fact that in a minority of verbs (contextually of perceiving etc.) the usual Standard English correspondent is, e.g., he thinks, more delicately still also is thinking in a less usual (co-textual/situational) use.

Finally, if we examined the linear correspondences (in compar-

[49] Halliday, "Categories", p. 272.
[50] Similarly, on a small scale, with phonological systems, as in the "prosodic" method of the London School advocated by Allen, op. cit., e.g. pp. 98–9 (and Ellis, "General . . .", pp. 156–8 [Appendix B, pp. 95–5]), but not explicitly by him in this specific connection. E.g. terms in Turkish systems of vowel (and consonant) prosody extend over the word (or part of it) (see N. Waterson, "Some Aspects of the Phonology of the Nominal Forms of the Turkish Word", Bulletin of the School of Oriental and African Studies, Vol. XVIII, 1956, pp. 578–91, especially pp. 579–81; also R. B. Lees, The Phonology of Modern Standard Turkish, The Hague, 1961, pp. 52–4, 10–15), and this should be taken into account in identifying phonological exponents in pairs like (Sandfeld, pp. 90–1) B. битисвам, T. bitti; B. батисвам, T. battı; beside (Sandfeld, p. 92) B. -лък, T. -lık.

able situations, including texts in translation-relation (cf. n. 31), on which systemic identifications are in principle ultimately based (cf. nn. 31, 47 and references in n. 48), greater frequency of occurrence of the terms in the system would make possible greater delicacy of discrimination among them, on the other scales, and in general a further scale of delicacy of extent of text represented would also be possible (but to reflect this last in quantification would require weighting of correspondences according to frequency, which is not attempted here).

Now given that say for example in English and Bulgarian (to take an instance (not necessarily relevant to areal community) of one language of each region) the systems of personal pronouns[51] ("nominatives" in the sense of excluding reflexive) can be shown to have terms corresponding as follows:

I: аз; *he/she/it*: той/тя/то (abstracting from the respective intersecting systems of "natural" and "grammatical" gender respectively); *we*: ние; *they*: те, leaving *you*, ти and вие without one-to-one correspondents,

then we have an English system of 5 terms, a Bulgarian of 6, aggregate 11, and reduced, "generic" (Allen, p. 90) system of 7 (4 correspondents (terms in one-to-one correspondence) plus 3).

The extent of correspondence is then expressed (Allen, p. 92) as proportional minority by dividing generic by aggregate, namely 7/11. Since this formula gives values between ½ (for complete correspondence, aggregate equals twice generic) and 1 (for complete non-correspondence, aggregate equals generic), to give a value between 0 and 1 we invert and[52] subtract 1, giving aggregate minus generic all divided by generic, in other words number of correspondents divided by generic, in this case 4/7.

Further statistical operations will be called for if and when individual values for individual systems and (relevant parts of) individual pairs of languages are accumulated, in order to give

[51]   Allen's own example of a system, "Relationship", p. 99.
[52]   This is Dixon's modification, which (besides having the numerator formulatable simply as number of correspondents) has the advantages over Ross's $\log_2$ of the inverted proportional minority (Allen, p. 93, n. 1) of dispensing with logarithms and of giving a straight line in the graph.

values for sets of systems and of languages and summations of values for pairs and sets of languages and of summations in "meta-comparison" (see n. 38). Dixon suggests for at least some of these as a method requiring no mathematical expertise (cf. n. 52) simply adding the fractional (between 0 and 1) values, and stating the total as for, or divided by, the number of systems, etc., in question.

E.g., if English-Bulgarian (equally indelicate (and excluding *my* etc. *own*)) possessive systems have, English 5, Bulgarian 7 (i.e. including свой), generic 8, giving 4/8, then for the set (of two) of (indelicate) systems personal pronouns ("nominatives") and possessives, we have "4/7 plus 4/8 for 2", equals "15/14 for 2" or "15/28".[53]

4. *Concluding Remarks*

Space forbids at this point multiplication of examples from systems in pairs of languages (of the two regions) that might be relevant to areal convergence. In any event, the evaluation of their relevance would depend upon large-scale, if not exhaustive, extension of the comparative statement throughout the languages – together with the establishing of the limits and proportions of the systemic and non-systemic.

The present paper argues the desirability of such research, but admits the magnitude of the tasks involved, both practical and theoretical.

---

[53] Note that this differs from the result if we aggregated the two generic systems and their correspondents, 7 plus 8 and 5 plus 4, which would give 8/15. Thus the distinction of one comparable pair of systems from another remains reflected.

Appendix G

ON COMPARATIVE DESCRIPTIVE LINGUISTICS*

Some attention has been paid recently to the question of developing a "comparative linguistics" more general than the genetic comparative linguistics of "comparative philology".[1]

For a comparative linguistics that has the rigour of contemporary descriptive linguistics comparison must be of specific languages in specific detail.[2] It does not matter what languages, from the point of view of method; certain purposes (such as demonstration of method) may be served better by certain choices.

This may be done by first making a description of each language from its texts, and then confronting comparable systems within each language.[3] But the question arises of establishing the com-

---

* My thanks are due for criticism and assistance to Dr. M. A. K. Halliday and Dr. P. Wexler.

[1] See W. S. Allen, "Relationship in Comparative Linguistics", *Transactions of the Philological Society*, 1953, pp. 52–108, and his bibliography (especially pp. 88–89), and my criticism, "General Linguistics and Comparative Philology", [Appendix B].

[2] According to Allen, *op. cit.*, pp. 90–93, by pairs of languages, with "quasi-mathematical" formulation, expressing degree of correspondence (of each system compared). Cf. N. I. Fel'dman's review of A. V. Fedorov's *Введение в теорию перевода*, in *Вопросы языкознания*, 1954, pp. 117–127 (p. 118).

[3] Allen, *op. cit.*, p. 90; M. A. K. Halliday, "Some Aspects of Systematic Description and Comparison in Grammatical Analysis" (to be published in the *Philological Society's Studies in Linguistic Analysis*). Cf. H. Pilch, reviewing H. Weber's *Das Tempussystem des Deutschen und des Französischen: Übersetzungs- und Strukturprobleme*, in *Language*, 31 (1955), pp. 130–133 (p. 130): "Conceiving of a given language as a self-contained structure and defining its units in terms of their mutual contrasts, each on its own level, we can compare units of different languages, now that they are no longer isolated, not by referring them to some extra-linguistic common denominator – but only as parts of their respective systems, i.e. by virtue of similar formal relations

parability of systems (Allen, *op. cit.*, p. 94). Phonological systems present no great difficulty.[4] But semantic systems set problems[5] the solution of which appears to be the finding of linguistic contexts referable to the same context of situation.[6]

Can translations provide such a means? A translation is the expression in one language of what has already been expressed in another; and the "*what* is expressed" constitutes the non-linguistic context to which both versions could be referred. The first difficulty is that this non-linguistic context as a whole is known, to the translator and the linguistic investigator, only through the original expression of it.[7] What in fact is expressed by any attempt at translation is one of the possible total non-linguistic contexts that could be understood from the original text, and one says that the attempt is a (good) translation to the extent that it conveys what is shown, by knowledge of the original language and its various contexts (i.e. other "texts" and their situations), to have been the original in-

---

between the units concerned and the total language structure"; Fedorov, *op. cit.*, p. 195 (quoted by Fel'dman, p. 120): "необходимость все время иметь в виду системы языковых средств, а не разрозненные или случайно выделенные элементы".

[4] Pilch, *op. cit.*, p. 130: "For instance, a statement to the effect that different languages have syllabic phonemes means that they have classes of sounds fitting similar formal definitions. Allen, *op. cit.*, p. 95–96.

[5] Allen, *op. cit.*, pp. 99–100, who does not make a complete classification of semantic functions, either into grammatical and lexical (and phonaesthetic, cf. p. 558, n. 2), or (which would illuminate his splitting of the formally grammatical (see n. 1), as Fel'dman (pp. 121, 122, 126) does, into "material content" and "logical content" (and "expressive content"; cf. I. A. Richards, *Speculative Instruments*, London, 1955, p. 27).

[6] As defined by J. R. Firth, referred to by Allen, p. 99, and Halliday, *op. cit.* Allen, p. 100, limits grammatical terms comparable by available methods to those where the identificatory function is non-grammatical (e.g. personal pronouns); Halliday shows that Allen's method can in fact be extended to other grammatical terms by cumulative identification of components of the linguistic context.

[7] В. А. Griftsov, "Заметки по технике перевода", *Вопросы языкознания*, 1952, 5, p. 86: "Трудность переводческого дела в том, что писатель видит вещи и затем их обозначает словом, переводчик же видит слова, за которыми обязан восстановить вещи". Pilch, *op. cit.*, p. 131: "The independent, nonfictional 'reality' chosen by (Weber) as his tertium comparationis does not exist. ... how could (Weber) possibly assess it, as long as his only knowledge of the one rests on the other?"

tention.[8] This then constitutes a second difficulty: the varying quality of "translations" (attempts at translation). A final difficulty is that in order to convey as much as possible of the original it may be necessary to use a style of the language of translation that, while wholly intelligible to the reader, is not a style used normally, i.e. for original composition.

All these things undoubtedly make the comparison of a text and its translation (or, even more so, of translations into different languages) a method of comparative linguistics better avoided, other things being equal. But other things seldom are equal; nor need the purposes be so comprehensive that complete certainty about the total non-linguistic context of one's texts is essential. For example, an exhaustive comparison of what C. Haag terms "Ausdruck der Denkordnung"[9] in German and Chinese would require a deep knowledge of each language and its situations,[10] such as one trusts Haag had before applying his categories; but for a comparison that merely sets out to demonstrate some of the diversity of structure in languages so removed from each other (and thereby throw into relief the specific character of German),[11] it should meet the purpose to take a translation of which it can be postulated that the second difficulty (the translator's command of the languages) is met,[12] any reservations due to the third difficulty (specific style of

[8] Fel'dman, op. cit., p. 125: "Перевод есть воспроизведение на другом языке мысли подлинника во всей полноте ее словарно-вещественного и логического содержания."

[9] C. Haag, "Ausdruck der Denkordnung im Chinesischen", Wörter und Sachen, neue Folge, III, (1940), pp. 1–25, "Ausdruck der Denkordnung im Deutschen", ibid., IV (1941–1942), pp. 1–17.

[10] Cf. Richards, op. cit., p. 20: "How may we compare what a sentence in English may mean with what a sentence in Chinese may mean? The only sound traditional answer is in terms of two scholarships – one in English, the other in Chinese."

[11] Cf. Fel'dman, op. cit., p. 121: "когда речь и дет о переводе с языка, близкого по структуре, трудности эти (технические трудности перевода) в одном отношении ограничены. ... в данный момент еще нет возможности строить теорию перевода на более широкой основе, поскольку пока нет никаких работ по обобщению опыта перевода с языков других систем ..."

[12] Cf. Pilch, op. cit., p. 133: "The conclusion – that in translations the ... forms used are those required by the context and the Sprachgefühl of the trans-

language of translation) being immaterial to the purpose; and what is left of the first difficulty, in what sense the two versions can be said to correspond, in the absence of a directly observable referent as "tertium comparationis" (cf. p. 155, n. 7), will be taken up in making the comparison.

Here then is a specimen of such texts. (The "translations" into English are parenthetic, as part of the apparatus of exposition and not as data for comparison. The transcription (Ladingxua Sinwenz)[13] of the Chinese character by character is likewise a mere device of exposition.)

"Ich habe diese Erzählungen nur um der besonderen Schönheit willen zusammengetragen, mit der sie mein Herz in früherem oder späterem Alter berührt haben und mir unvergesslich geworden sind, so dass ich, um sie aneinanderzureihen, keines Hilfsmittels bedurfte als meines Gedächtnisses." (H. von Hofmannsthal, *Deutsche Erzähler*)

("I have collected these stories together only for the sake of the particular beauty with which they have touched my heart in my younger or older years and have become unforgettable to me, so that in order to compile them I have needed no other help than my memory.")

"wǒ bǎ zhè sie siǎo shuō zí zài ì kǐ, žh wèi liao nà tè shū d měi, tā mn ỳng zhè zhung měi xuì gīng zài zǎo nián xuò wǎn nián gǎn dùng le wǒ d sīn, wǒ nán ý wàng kyò, žh šh wǒ rhú gīn biān pái tā mn chú kyò wǒ d gì ì bìng bù sỹ iào kí tā d bāng zhù" (Feng Chih's translation).

("It is simply for their particular beauty that I have assembled these stories, a beauty with which both in my youth and in later years they have always been able to move me; I could never forget them, and indeed in compiling them now I need no other help than my own memory."[14])

---

lator . . . should have been among the author's preliminary assumptions if his choice of sources was to make any sense at all."

[13] [In the transcription used above (n. 66 on p. 55): – Wo ba zhexie xiaoshuo ji zai yiqi, zhi weiliao na teshude mei, tamen yong zhezhong mei hui jing zai zaonian huo wannian gandongle wode xin, wo nanyu wangque, zhi shi wo rujin bianpai tamen chuque wode jiyi bing bu xuyao qitade bangzhu.]

[14] This translation was kindly made by Dr. Halliday without reference to the German.

It is apparent to anyone who knows Chinese that the Chinese text is a translation, and to anyone who knows both languages it is apparent from the German text alone that it could not be a translation from Chinese. But the one is Chinese as much as the other is German; and it expresses to someone understanding Chinese more or less what the other expresses to someone understanding German. (How more and less will be discussed in the conclusions.)

Now each passage conveys what it does because it is made up of components known already from other contexts,[15] e.g. *schön* in *schönes Wetter* ("fine weather", Chinese *mei miao tian ki*), etc. (and cf. Hofmannsthal's own essay "Schöne Sprache"); *sin* in *i sin gung zo* ("put one's heart into one's work"), etc. These other contexts would not be translated using the same component every time for this component,[16] e.g. to *sin*, here *Herz*, often corresponds *Geist*. None the less, to this component and no other may be said to correspond in this passage that component in the other language which from other contexts is given this translation among others.

It is on such a basis that "meanings" of terms or expressions consisting of one or more words or characters are listed in bilingual dictionaries. But these, lexical meanings, are not the *only* components of the "meaning" of a text. There are also "grammatical meanings", attributable to combinations of words and characters and to meaningful units less than words.

There are of course no such divisions within the Chinese character. (There are in spoken Chinese, and in Ladingxua Sinwenz orthography, divisions corresponding to words in German (or other languages with alphabetical script) and consisting of one or more characters; but these are not marked in a text written with characters.) There are indeed graphic divisions of the character,

---

[15] Cf. Richards, *op. cit.*, p. 23: "The comprehending of any utterance is guided by any number of partially similar situations in which partially similar utterances have occurred." Whether consciously or not, one's basis of comparison is always ultimately derived from experience of contexts of situation. Even Haag's "tertium comparationis", *der logische Bau der Denkordnung*, is an attempted abstraction from the situations of any language.

[16] For an attempt to systematize these variations for German and English see E. Leisi, *Der Wortinhalt, seine Struktur im Deutschen und Englischen* (Heidelberg, 1953).

e.g. the character for *wo* ("I") consists of a graph identifiable as the character for *i* ("one") and that for *shou* ("hand") (or according to some, the fuller form of *shou* alone) and that for *go* ("spear"), just as there are phonetic divisions of the spoken language, e.g. w + o + falling-rising tone or German ʔ + short i + ç, or graphic divisions (letters) in the German, e.g. i + c + h. But these are not meaningful units,[17] and therefore[18] not ones that could correspond one-to-one with the other language. Thus the minimum meaningful unit in Chinese is the character. In German, however, words may consist of smaller meaningful units, which is usually expressed by saying that German words may be derived from others, e.g. *Erzählung* from *erzählen*, and may have more than one form, e.g. *Erzählung/Erzählungen.* (Thus what corresponds[19] in German to the character (other than graphically[20]) is something less than a word, and in spoken Chinese and LS too words may be derived from other words, e.g. *siao shuo* (LS *siaoshuo*), "story", from *siao* "small" and *shuo*, "speak", or have more than one form, e.g. *wo/wo d* (LS *wod*) paralleling (semantically) German *ich/mein.*)

The following are the divisions of this kind in the German, with alternative forms (mostly not occurring here) of the words to demonstrate their divisibility, and with the division between parts constituting derivation from other words distinguished by dash instead of hyphen:

---

[17] In poetic (verse or prose) translation, especially between closely related languages (e.g. English and Dutch), there might be correspondence of phonaesthemes (cf. J. R. Firth on phonaesthetics, e.g. in "Modes of Meaning", *Essays and Studies of the English Association*, 1951), i.e. phonetic units with "meaning" abstracted from phonetically similar lexical units. In Pound's verse "translations" of classical Chinese, lexical functions of English words are used to correspond to some of the Chinese graphic divisions.

[18] Or rather, in terms of the present comparative analysis, since there is no such correspondence, there is no reason to consider them meaningful.

[19] i.e. corresponds in general (as minimum meaningful unit, "morpheme"), and may "correspond" in translation.

[20] Graphically there is no one unit corresponding to the character, since the relevant dimensions of the graphic system contain different numbers of terms in the two languages (non-successive units: strokes in both, graphs in Chinese only; successive units: letters/characters; units separated by space/regularity of succession: words/characters).

hab-e (haben); dies-e (dieser); Er – zähl – ung-en (Erzählung); d-er (die); be – sonder-en (besonderer); zusammen – ge-trag-en (trage zusammen / zusammentrage); früh-er-em (früher, früh), so späterem; be – rühr-t (berühren); ge-word-en (werde); an – ein – ander – zu-reih-en (reihe aneinander /aneinanderreihe); kein-es (kein); Hilf-s – mitt – el-s (Hilfsmittel), so Ge – dächt – niss-es; be – durf-te (bedarf).

To these may be added forms with zero component here, alternating with other components:

Schön – heit (Schönheit-en); mein (mein-es); Herz (Herz-en); Alt – er (Alter-s); un – vergess – lich (unvergesslich-e)
and forms not divisible formally (not at least with the same facility as the above) but of divisible meaning paralleling the above:

ich/mir/mein- (paralleling e.g. die/der/der); sie/er, sie, es (paralleling Erzählungen/Erzählung); sind/bin (paralleling haben/habe); and -word-/werd- (paralleling -rühr-t/ (-) rühr-en).

Just as these forms are semantically divisible without being formally so, so may the smaller meaningful units be, e.g. the -es in *Gedächtnisses* means both "genitive" and "singular", i.e. *Gedächtnisses* alternates on the one hand with *Gedächtnis* nominative/ accusative/ dative singular and on the other with *Gedächtnisse* genitive plural.

The above functions of German minimum meaningful units are paralleled in Chinese characters, including zero component, e.g. *wo* beside *wo mn* ("we"), but not semantic divisibility without formal divisibility (like German *ich/wir*, unless one so regards *za mn*, "we" inclusive of the person(s) addressed (but see below on *ich/wo* (correspondence-unit no. 2)) or the negative imperative *bie* (cf. p. 167)). From zero component may be distinguished absence of an optional category,[21] e.g. those nouns like *xyo sheng* which may have a plural like *xyo sheng mn*, without the *mn* are not, like the personal pronouns, singular, but are numberless.

The characters in the Chinese then complete the inventory of

---

[21] It might be argued that the latter is equally zero form, with a more *merk-mallos* function; but for present purposes at least it is convenient to make this terminological distinction.

components of which correspondence, whether one-to-one or complex, is possible – with the exception of a component of another kind: the way in which the words or characters[22] are put together, their order and grouping. It is now possible to examine how these make up divisions of the texts that correspond.

Correspondence of a division of the one text with a division of the other may be established by varying the one and seeing whether the other would change. E.g. the whole German passage above could be replaced (within the work of which it forms part), and then the whole Chinese passage would have to be replaced; or just the first character of the Chinese could be replaced, say by *ni* ("you"), and then the German would replace *ich . . . -e* (in *habe . . . zusammengetragen*) by *Sie . . . -en*.

Minimum units of correspondence may be established by finding the smallest such variations. E.g. *ich . . . -e/wo* (or rather (cf. below, correspondence-units 1.–4.) *ich* plus one meaning in this position) cannot be further divided linearly: as far as the use of *wo* here is concerned, *wo* corresponds to two German linear sections; from other uses one can say that in general it corresponds to (the person-number meaning of) the one linear section *ich* (cf. without *wo/ich, cing/bitt-e* ("/I/ request"), "please"). Thus minimum units of correspondence are no smaller than and may be larger than minimum units of one language as arrived at above. The significance of the relation of the two classes of unit will form part of the conclusions. Meanwhile units of the latter class are assumed to be already established.[23]

---

[22] So far (apart from the reference to spoken Chinese) "words" have been defined orthographically (cf. p. 159, n. 20); in fact, the word (in either language) could be defined as the unit of order and grouping, since within a given word the order of morphemes is fixed (any forms differing only in this being distinct words). In this sense of "words", "or characters" could be omitted here. (But there are exceptions to the coterminousness of words in the two senses, e.g. forms like *zusammentrage* cited above.)

[23] For German, cf. H. Glinz, *Die Innere Form des Deutschen* (Berne, 1952); for Chinese, e.g. Wang Liao-I, *Основы Китайской Грамматики*, edited by A. A. Dragunov (Moscow, 1954) [or M. A. K. Halliday, "Grammatical Categories in Modern Chinese", *TPS* (1956), pp. 177–244].

The following are the minimum divisions of meaning corresponding in the two versions:

1. To the "first person"[24] meaning of *ich* . . . *-e* corresponds *wo*.

2. The opposition of *wo* to *wo mn*, *za mn*, formally of singular to plural, corresponds to the difference between *ich* . . . *-e* and *wir* . . . *-en* which there is no formal reason for regarding as singular and plural *of the same* lexical unit.[25] So that either the two Chinese units (*wo*; absence of *mn*) can be regarded as one correspondence-unit (corresponding to the one German unit *ich* (. . . *-e*), opposed on the same level to *Sie*, etc. and *wir* (. . . *-en*, etc.)), or the German can be regarded as a. first person (corresponding: *wo-*) and therefore b. singular (corresponding: zero). (In either case *wir* is regarded as a. not *only* first person, because b. plural, and according as a. in a given context is not necessarily inclusive of second person (*wo-*, cf. n. 25) or is, the Chinese corresponding is the plural of an existing singular pronoun (*wo mn*) or not (*za mn*).)

3. To the nominative form of *ich* with a verb of the *zusammentragen* type corresponds the position of *wo* before the verb expression *zi zai i ki*. (One cannot simply equate nominative in "subject"-use with any verb in German with position before any verb in Chinese, since the lexical meaning of the verbs in some corresponding translation-contexts is such that to the "subject" in one language corresponds something other than a "subject" in the other language, e.g. *Regen fällt* ("rain falls") /*xia y* ("/it/ drops rain"); conversely, in our passage, *wo nan y wang kyo/mir unvergesslich geworden sind* (which see (no. 39) on the problem of scope of correspondence). This is quite a different matter from equating "nominatives" for genetic-linguistic purposes (where, for one

---

[24]   Glinz, *op. cit.*, p. 109: "sprechend".

[25]   As even Glinz does (p. 109, "sprechend Einzahl, sprechend Mehrzahl"), though he does say "Dabei darf man auch hier mit der Genauigkeit der Parallelisierung nicht weiter gehen, als es die Sprache selber tut. So ist 'wir wollen' in strengem Sinne doppelt interpretierbar; die vielen Wollenden können alle zusammen sprechen, also im Chor, oder es kann einer im Namen aller sprechen und trotzdem sagen: 'wir wollen'." – in fact, is not the former (which incidentally would be *wo mn* in the forms of Chinese distinguishing *za mn*) a special case (each speaker a case) of the latter (equally *wo mn*)?

thing, some of the verbs concerned are genetically identical), cf. Allen, p. 79 and my criticism (see p. 154, n. 1).)

4. To the "present"[26] meaning of -e in *habe* and the "perfect"[27] meaning of *hab- . . . -ge- -en* there is nothing corresponding – the Chinese here is uncharacterized (cf. p. 559, n. 1) as to temporal categories (contrast *gan dung le*, n. 34), cf. n. 27.

5. To *zusammen- -trag-* corresponds *zi zai i ki*.

6. To *dies-* corresponds *zhe*.

7. To the plural meaning of -e in *diese* corresponds *sie* (plural "classifier" beside *go*, etc. singular).

8. To *Erzählung-* corresponds *siao shuo*.

9. To the plural meaning of *-en* in *Erzählungen* there is nothing corresponding other than no. 7, *sie* being taken there with -e since they would remain if *Erzählungen/siao shuo* were omitted, though -e would not then be unambiguously plural without further context; on the other hand this is the only kind of way in which plurality could be indicated with *siao shuo*, one of the vast majority of nouns never having *mn* (because not personal).

10. *ba* before *zi zai i ki* (with a verb of this type[28]) corresponds to the accusative meaning with a verb of *zusammentragen* type of -e in *diese* (*-en* in *Erzählungen* has no case-oppositions like *dieser, diesen*) shown (as not nominative) by *ich* being nominative, *habe* being singular, and the lexical context.

11. The non-emphatic position of *ba zhe sie siao shuo*[29] before

[26] Glinz, *op. cit.*, p. 103: "allgemein".

[27] H. Garey, *The Historical Development of Tenses from Late Latin to Old French* (= *Language Dissertation*, No. 51) (1955), p. 13: "anterior tempus" (event before reference period), here combined with "present" "tense" (Garey, p. 12: relationship of reference period to speech moment) giving "vollzogen" Glinz, *op. cit.*, p. 360, beside "vorvollzogen", anterior tempus of "(nur) ver-gangen" tense (*hatte- ge- -en*) "chrone" (Garey, p. 13: relationship of event, reference period and speech moment), which since "present" is not restricted to the present (*allgemein*) amounts to general anterior "chroneme" (Garey, p. 14: meaning of a set common to its chrones in various utterances), here chrone "prelocutory" "action" (Garey, p. 13; "the relationship of event to speech moment (specified only when tense is not explicit in a form or utterance)"), cf. no. 34.

[28] Wang, *op. cit.*, p. 122.

[29] i.e. of *zhe sie siao shuo*, made possible by making it grammatically the object of subordinate (therefore pre-main-verb) verb *ba*. Wang, *op. cit.*, p. 120.

the verb (cf. no. 10) expressing[30] that the former is the given, part of psychological[31] subject (with *wo*), and the latter the new, the psychological predicate, corresponds to *diese Erzählungen* is not being in emphatic position (changing places with grammatical subject); English would express this by normal actor-action order read without emphasis of the object or by passive without specification of logical subject (which would otherwise be in emphatic position): "these stories have been collected together" (without "by me").

12. To *um . . . willen* plus genitive meaning of *-er -en* in *der besonderen* corresponds *wei liao* before *na . . .*

13. To *d-* corresponds *na*.

14. To *besonder-* corresponds *te shu d*.

15. To *Schönheit-* plus the feminine meaning of *-er* in *der*[32] corresponds *mei*.

16. To the singular meaning of – in *Schönheit* corresponds nothing, cf. no. 9.[33]

---

[30] Wang, *op. cit.*, pp. 121, 248. Halliday (unpublished thesis): "In fact, probably because of its stress correlation, contextual reference to given/new is often termed 'emphasis'."; cf., for the spoken (stress) reflected, C. Hockett, "Peiping Morphophonemics", *Language*, 26, 1950, pp. 62–85 (pp. 67–68).

[31] Fel'dman, *op. cit.*, p. 122: part of "logical content"; by Halliday referred (cf. p. 154, n. 3) to "context of mention".

[32] Glinz, *op. cit.*, p. 269 ff. Cf. C. Bazell, "Analogical System", *Transactions of the Philological Society*, 1938, pp. 104 ff. (p. 114); V. Skalička, "O Jazykové Subsumaci", *Časopis pro Moderní Filologii*, XXVI, pp. 24 ff. (pp. 26–27).

[33] Cf. Glinz, *op. cit.*, p. 152: "Ist an einem Bilde vieles schön, so spricht man von seinen 'Schönheiten'. Will man das 'schön' als *eines* zusammenfassen, so ist es die 'Schönheit'", which seems to be a case of literally meta-linguistic thinking. (Cf. B. Whorf's "Essays on Metalinguistics"; Whorf however would equally attribute the "thought" to the ordinary speaker's collocations, not the grammarian's interpretation of them. See the refutation of Whorf's conception of "linguistic thinking" by M. M. Gukhman, *Вопросы языкознания* (1954), 1, p. 124 – in general, Gukhman's criticism of Whorf (pp. 122–127) seems to me not to bring out sufficiently Whorf's implicit denial of the progress in thought represented by modern ("European") science (cf. J. Whatmough, *Preliminary Reports*, Seventh International Congress of Linguists, London, 1952, p. 26: "Whorf was wrong, for example, in declaring that Newtonian physics is a mere recept from language, as if (notwithstanding the fact of nuclear fission) modern physics were a linguistic invention!").)

17. To *mit* plus the dative meaning of *-er* in *der* corresponds *yng* before *zhe* . . .

18. To the "relative pronoun" meaning of *d-* plus final position of verb plus the reference to *Schönheit* shown by the feminine meaning of *-er* corresponds *zhe zhung mei.*

19. For the singular meaning of *-er* with *mit* cf. no. 16.

20. To the third person meaning of *sie* . . . *-en* corresponds the third person meaning of *ta.*

21. To the plural meaning of *sie* . . . *-en* corresponds *mn.*

22. The neuter meaning of *ta* (i.e. character with ox-radical, as opp. man-, (LS "taa") woman-radical) corresponds to nothing (except the lexical nature of *Erzählungen*) in the German (if German plural showed gender, the reference to the noun shown by the Chinese neuter ("natural gender") would correspond to the reference to the noun shown by the German feminine ("grammatical gender").

23. To the first person (cf. nos. 1. and 2., p. 162, nn. 24 and 25) meaning in *mein* (cf. Glinz, *op. cit.*, p. 300) corresponds *wo.*

24. To the possessive meaning in *mein* corresponds *d.*

25. To *Herz* plus the neuter meaning of – in *mein* corresponds *sin.*

26. To the singular meaning of – . . . – in *mein Herz* corresponds nothing.

27. To the fact that *mein Herz* is object with a verb of *berühren* type (cf. no. 3) shown by the verb's being plural corresponds the position of *wo d sin* after a verb of *gan dung* type.

28. To *in* plus the dative meaning of *-em* corresponds *ging zai* (*ging* specifically corresponding to the temporal nature of the context specified only lexically in the German).

29. and 30. To *früh-* and *spät-* plus the "Höherstufe" meaning (Glinz, *op. cit.*, pp. 195–196) of *-er-* correspond *zao* and *wan.*

31. To *oder* corresponds *xuo.*

32. To *Alter* singular plus the singular neuter meaning of *-em* corresponds *nian* numberless (cf. nos. 9, 16, 19).

33. To *berühr-* corresponds *gan dung.*

34. To the "perfect" (p. 163, n. 27) meaning of *-t hab-* plus the "present" (p. 163, n. 26) meaning of *-en* corresponds the prelocu-

tory chrone (p. 163, n. 27) of the combination of prelocutory chroneme of *le* after verb (as opp. *le* clause-final, aspect[34]) and *xui* lexically specifying bare prelocutory.

35. To *und* corresponds mere juxtaposition of the clauses.

36. To the first person meaning in *mir* corresponds *wo*.

37. To the lexical elements *un- -lich* plus dative form of *mir* plus the verbal (copula) force of *geworden sind* corresponds *nan y* plus subject position of *wo*.

38. To *-vergess-* corresponds *wang kyo*.

39. To the Aktionsart of *-werd-* (beside simple copula *sein*) plus chrone (p. 163, n. 27) of *ge- -en* (with *-o-*) *sind* and to the person and number of *sind* corresponds nothing, the clause-structures being in any case incommensurable, so that the correspondences in no. 37 are a rougher approximation than most of the units.

40. To *so dass* corresponds *zh sh*.

41–43. For *ich/who* see nos. 1–3; 1–2 also for part of the meaning of *-te* (53).

44. To *um . . . -zu- -en* corresponds the position of *bian pai* before *sy iao* (cf. p. 561, n. 2).

45–47. For *sie/ta mn* see nos. 20–22.

48. To *aneinander- -reih-* corresponds *bian pai*.

49. To *kein- . . . als* (plus genitive meaning of *-es -es*) corresponds *chu kyo* (before *gi i*) . . . *bing bu . . . ki ta d*.

50. To *Hilfsmittel-* corresponds *bang zhu*.

51. To the singular meaning of *-es -s* corresponds nothing.

52. To *bedurf-* plus the genitive meaning of *-es -s* corresponds *sy iao* before *bang zhu*.

53. To the past meaning (cf. p. 163, n. 27) of *-te* (cf. no. 43) corresponds nothing.

54–55. For *mein-/wo d* see nos. 23–24.

56. To *Gedächtniss-* plus neuter meaning of *-es* in *meines* corresponds *gi i*.

57. To the singular meaning of *-es -es* corresponds nothing.

In the above no mention has been made of voice or mood, all the German verbs here being in the "active" and the "indicative". The

[34] in Garey's sense (*op. cit.*, p. 13); subdivision of simple tempus.

voice-meaning is in fact subsumed in the clause-structure, dependent partly on the lexical character of the verb,[35] referred to in
nos. 3, 10–11, 27, 39, 52. But to a modal morpheme-meaning in
German can sometimes be found corresponding a Chinese morpheme, e.g. komme nicht!/bu iao lai (alternatively komme nicht!/
bie lai), or part of a Chinese morpheme-meaning, e.g. (besides bie
above) er wird kommen; sie denken, er werde kommen/ta iao lai;
ta mn siang ta xui lai.

Now it is clear enough that the "correspondence-units" abstracted from the two versions do not represent precise correspondence
of "meaning" each to each; they constitute a corresponding meaning
only it relation to the rest of the units (and ultimately to the whole
text – which conveys what it does, as was said, because it is made up
of such components but equally because it is made up, because the
components are put together (into something new)[36]).[37]

In no. 32, for example, it is to a combination of certain German
adjectives with Alter ("age") that a combination of certain Chinese
adjectives with nian ("year (s)") corresponds. Or in no. 44, in itself
the Chinese does not express purpose as the German here does while
other German constructions corresponding elsewhere to the same
Chinese construction (cf. nos. 10–11 (p. 163, n. 29) or chu kyo in
no. 49) do not; but what is expressed in German by specifying
purpose is gathered from the whole Chinese passage without its
being specified by particular morphemes.

Thus the Chinese can be said to express both less (when its unit
is less specific a term in a series of fewer terms, e.g. nos. 4, 9, 16, 19,
26, 35, 39, 51, 53, 56) and more (e.g. no. 3 on za mn, nos. 11, 18, 22,
28, 34, 49) in its discrete units, but these unevennesses of fit are
submerged in the correspondence of the whole – a correspondence
of as it were the focal point of reference, notwithstanding any
divergent cultural overtones, e.g. the differing attitudes to age that

[35] Wang, op. cit., p. 127.
[36] Cf. W. Haas, Seventh Congress (op. cit. in. p. 561, n. 6), p. 26 ("Speech is a
creative process capable of presenting what is not present in any one of its parts,
nor distributed over all."); Glinz, op. cit., p. 38, on the "Zweiklassensystem".
[37] Cf. Fel'dman, op. cit., pp. 121, 122, 125.

may be evoked by the whole concept expressed at nos. 29–32.[38]
(To vary the image, it is as if what at viewing distance appeared an
identical plane pattern were found to be projected by a volume
of differing composition.)

Nevertheless, while always remembering the relativity of the
significance of the discrete correspondence-units on the level of
stylistics, it is of interest to linguistic theory to examine their relation to the units of the single language. With so short a specimen
absolute statistics are of little value, e.g. the fact that out of the
fifty-seven items listed there are half a dozen cases of one-to-one
morpheme correspondence or three of two (successive) corresponding to two. What *is* significant is: of the large number of items
where at least one version has a complex unit and/or includes only
a part of the meaning of a formal division, how much more often
it is the German that does so.

On such a basis one can list a number of distinguishing characteristics of German structure:

1. In general, relations between formal divisions and meaning-
divisions are more complex than in Chinese.

2. Meanings are cumulated in formal divisions in a majority of
grammatical morphemes, beside very rarely in Chinese.

3. The same formal units (*-e, -en, -er*, etc.) are found for various
combinations of grammatical meanings (Glinz, *op. cit.*, p. 124:
"Systemplätze") and asymmetrically distributed over and as between paradigms.

4. It therefore often happens that a grammatical meaning is
made specific only by a linear combination of forms from differing
paradigms (e.g. no. 12, cf. nos. 9, 19).

5. The expression of grammatical categories is not optional, as
often in Chinese.

6. Word-order is not simply correlated with internal clause-

---

[38]   Cf. F. Boillot, *Le vrai ami du traducteur* (Paris, 1930), pp. 7–10, on the image
of navvies having their breakfast / des terrassiers en train de déjeuner. E. Nida,
"Linguistics and Ethnology in Translation-Problems" (*Word* I, 1945, pp. 194–
208), p. 194: "The person who is engaged in translating from one language to
another ought to be constantly aware of the contrast in the entire range of culture
represented by the two languages." Fel'dman, pp. 120, 122, 124, 125, 127.

structure, as in Chinese, but is partly fixed according to the place of the clause in the sentence-structure (e.g. no. 18), partly free to express psychological subject and predicate (cf. no. 11) in a more complex way than Chinese. The complex relation of order to meaning (including Glinz's "Prinzip der Endnähe = innerlichen Leitgliednähe"[39]) parallels the relative arbitrariness in the previous points.

7. Words are derived not only by composition (no. 50) as in Chinese, but by affixation (nos. 8, 33) much more elaborately than in Chinese (nos. 14, 15, 37). Thus in lexis too there is complexity of relation of form and meaning (general lexical complexity is another question).

(Points 3 and 4, and the actual extent of 2, are what are commonly referred to as "inflectional" features; 5 is what distinguishes both "inflectional" and "agglutinative" systems from "isolating", better termed "grouping" (P. Meriggi), systems, 7 also "stem-isolating" from fully "isolating".)

Thus a language like Chinese is a convenient choice for comparison with German – and Chinese itself (a well as being practically the most important language of its structural type) also because of the morphemic nature of its traditional writing.

This then is one procedure of descriptive linguistic comparison, which appears to justify itself for the particular purposes envisaged. (It may be described as linear or simple textual comparison.) To return to the question asked a the outset – can translations provide a means of referring linguistic contexts to the same context of situation (and thereby contribute to the more general techniques of comparative descriptive linguistics, concerned with comparison (of systems) abstracted from text)? – it is now evident that they can do so within certain limits. Verification of the quality of an attempt at translation, i.e. how far it does "correspond" to the original, is, while usually carried out through "practical knowledge" of both languages,[40] theoretically dependent upon some technique of

<hr>

[39]   p. 142, "der innerliche gliedmässige Zusammenhang tritt der räumlich-linearen Verteilung gewissermassen als Gegenspannung gegenüber."
[40]   Cf. Richards, *op. cit.*, p. 24: "It is not necessary that the members of a com-

establishing the reference[41] of each component in each.[42] Thus translation could never be the ultimate criterion of reference. None the less, given the prior establishment of the reference of components easy to establish by context of directly observable situation ("ostensive definition"), e.g. *zusammen- -trag-/zi zai i ki,* the possible reference (general, abstracted from text, "correspondence") of other components could well be stated by an accumulation of translation-contexts and a systemic interpretation of them. Both the collection of such data for given pairs of languages, and the elaboration of an adequate theory and technique of interpretation constitute formidable tasks; so do all aspects of the future work of developing comparative descriptive linguistics. It is hoped that the foregoing will have made some small contribution to suggesting a field for the further development of the science of linguistics which owes so much to Professor Mladenov.

---

parison-field – widely diverse utterances-within-situations as they may be – should ever have been taken together in explicit analytic scrutiny and examined as to their likenesses and differences . . . It is as though the nervous system had been taught Mill's Joint Method of Agreement and Difference."

[41] In the case of some grammatical units (including word-order), the "logical content" (p. 155, n. 5).

[42] Cf. p. 155, n. 6.

JANUA LINGUARUM

STUDIA MEMORIAE NICOLAI VAN WIJK DEDICATA

Edited by C. H. van Schooneveld

SERIES MINOR

MOUTON & CO . PUBLISHERS . THE HAGUE